CW00411283

WISDOM FOR LIVING

Volume Two
Daily Bible Reading Notes.

Martyn Perry

TABLE OF CONTENTS

INTRODUCTION

God speaks to us in the Scriptures, His written Word. It is so important to spend time each day with God reading our Bibles and praying. When we do this, we are able to understand what He has said, and seek Him about what this might mean for us in our daily lives.

In this book, Wisdom for Living, Volume Two, we look together at some of the Scriptures. These include what John has to say about seven signs Jesus performed (John 2:1-12:50), Roman justice and God's response (Mark 14:1-16:20), a selection of Psalms, the Ten Commandments, and the Book of Ruth.

As we spend time looking at God's Word we will hear Him speaking into our lives in a way that only He can.

SONGS OF WORSHIP AND LIFE

Onwards and Upwards
Read Psalm 121

In this section, we are going to look together at some of the most well-known Psalms.

This particular Psalm is called "A Song of Ascents." This possibly means that it's something that might have been on the lips of the Children of Israel on their way up to Jerusalem. There they would be able to worship appropriately at the Temple. It's significant that this song begins by thinking about the hills. Then the big question is asked about where real help can be found.

Some think that the hills being thought about are the mountains elsewhere in Israel which were associated with the giving of worship to the Canaanite fertility gods Baal or Asherah. What went on at such shrines was basically a semi-religious form of prostitution, namely the sex-trafficking of the daughters of Israel. When this was the official religion of the northern country of Israel, it was promoted by the royal family, and organized by the priests who administered these places.

3

We can only imagine what the reality of this would have been for one of Israel's teenage girls had they been taken to such a place by force. Added to this, such a religion also required families to sacrifice their young children to the gods, by throwing them alive into the flames. That's what so many people were doing, as their new "normal."

Others think that the mountains being thought about were associated with Jerusalem, which was on extremely high ground. It was there that the Temple could be found. Going up to it would really have been quite a climb. For such a trek, pilgrims would have been careful to wear their Fitbit to record the triumph, had such tech been available then. On the climb, the psalmist celebrates the faithfulness of God and His covenant love for His people. With each step of the journey, the psalmist, in effect, affirmed "I'll worship the Holy One of Israel, not Baal or Asherah. I'll trust in Him alone. As a family, we'll commit ourselves to holiness and to walking in God's ways. We'll only look to Him for help in times of need."

That's a costly affirmation, especially if others were making the opposite journey, a journey which was encouraged by the idolatrous Kings of Israel. No, this worshipper recognized God alone as King. He alone is the Creator, and He alone would protect. He would always be available to help and bless. This Psalm reminds us that when others look elsewhere in life for help and protection, we are invited to find our sense of protection and security in God, and only in Him.

Whatever is going on in our lives at the moment, this Psalm is such a treasure, and such an encouragement. It reminds us that God is always there for us. Even if others are beating a path to all sorts of other doors, perhaps doors that are considered cool and trendy, we'll only look to God for protection. He is our guard, the One who keeps us, and He never sleeps on the job. As we journey onwards and upwards with God day by day, we can look to Him. He'll always be there for us, and we can depend upon that.

Our Light and our Salvation

Read Psalm 27

This is a Psalm of David, though unlike other Psalms associated with him, we're not given a link between this song of praise and a particular episode in his life. So, we don't know when this was written, and we don't know exactly what he was facing in his life at the time. What we do know is that before he goes on to think specifically about what's troubling him (verses 7-14), he prays about his trust in God (verses 1-6).

David asks that God would hear him and be merciful to him as he prays. Others might forsake David, but he has this sense that God never will. He wants to walk in God's way, and asks that God will rescue him from his enemies. Even though we don't know what his enemies are doing against him, David does affirm his confidence that he can wait for God to act on his behalf. Perhaps he ends up expressing this confidence in the Lord, because he begins this Psalm where he does.

David begins by reminding himself that he doesn't need to fear any enemies, because the Lord is his light and his salvation (verse 1). His focus and intense longing is to be in the place where God is worshipped in the safety of His tabernacle (verse 5). This is the place where the Temple would eventually be built by his son, King Solomon. But for now, the portable tabernacle which was once used for worship in the wilderness is there as the place of worship.

It's a wonderful thing to know that God is beautiful (verse 4); what a privilege it is to be loved by such a God. We can look to Him, and this is a decision we can make, even when the ugliness of human sin and malice might be evident all around us.

No-one is asking us to pretend that all in the garden's rosy when we know we face obstacles and opposition. This isn't a Psalm which invites us to deny the reality of our situation. But it does invite us to make God, rather than our problem, our focus. True, we sometimes go through some hair-raising things. No-one is denying that. But we really can go through this time of testing and come out rejoicing on the other side of it. This doesn't happen by dumb luck, however. It can only happen when we choose not to talk incessantly about ourselves and our problems. Instead, we decide to focus on the One who can do something decisive to help us.

The Lord is our light and our salvation. He is our strong tower of support and protection (verse 1). He can lift us up above our problem and give us stability once more (verse 5). Whatever others might be doing to me in their malice, in the light of this Psalm, I'm invited to know that they don't have the final word over me or my life. God does, and God alone. And He wants to see me live a victorious life (verse 6). More than that, He can make this victory a reality in my life.

The Lord's Messiah

Read Psalm 110

This is a Psalm which is mentioned so many times in the Gospels and the Letters in Scripture. It was obviously an important Psalm for those who wrote about Jesus in later centuries.

One of the reasons for this is that Jesus understood this Psalm to refer to the Messiah (Matthew 22:41-46), the One who is greater than simply being a human descendant of King David. In the light of the sacrificial death and resurrection of Jesus, the first believers in Him were absolutely certain that this Messianic Psalm pointed forward to Jesus Himself. He had defeated sin, death and every spiritual enemy that could ever come against us.

When we face difficulties in life, the person who wrote the Letter to the Hebrews invites us to focus on Jesus (Hebrews 12:1-3). He sat down at the right hand of God (Hebrews 12:2; Psalm 110:1), having focussed on the victory which awaited Him after His faithful offering for sin on the Cross. In Hebrews, then, we are encouraged to persevere, ourselves. And the picture language at the start of Hebrews 12 is so wonderful. In chapter 11, the writer mentioned the heroes of faith, of whom we read in the writings of Moses and the Prophets. They are now "a great cloud of witnesses" (Hebrews 12:1), and they cheer us on from Heaven as we run our race with perseverance. What a wonderful thought.   In the light of all of this, in these verses from Psalm 110 and Hebrews 12:1-3, we know a number of things which are worth thinking about.

Jesus has won the decisive victory for us over sin. He persevered all the way to the Cross, because He focussed on the joy that was to come. We are cheered on by all the heroes of whom we read in Scripture. They have completed their race and have experienced God's victory in their own lives. We can do the same too. We know that when we pray about our difficulties, we do so knowing that our life's story reaches its climax in Heaven, where we participate fully in the victory of Jesus.

To Him, our Lord has said: "Sit at my right hand, until I make your enemies your footstool" (Psalm 110:1). The divine power which raised Jesus from the dead, and seated Him at the Father's right hand, is also at work in us here and now, whatever we face. We read of this in the Letter to the Ephesians (1:18-21). Things do come against us, that's true enough. But a great power is at work in us, which defies any comparison. This means that we are not simply fighting on our own using our own resources. We have within us the power that defeated death, conquered sin, and raised Jesus to the highest Heaven. We live daily under His great and almighty rule (Psalm 110:2). In Jesus the Messiah, we are on the winning team.

Two Ways
Read Psalm 1

Lots of people believe that this Psalm stands as an Introduction to the Book of Psalms as a whole. As it does, it holds before us a particular idea, the concept of "Torah." This seems to be central to our understanding of these songs of praise as a whole; it certainly is of this first one.

But firstly, what does the Hebrew word "Torah" mean? It tends to mean "Teaching, Instruction or Guidance" namely the teaching God gave to Moses in the first five books of the Bible. We need to keep the meaning of this word before us, because so many of our Christian translations of the Bible tend to render "Torah" as "Law," which can be a tad misleading. The Psalms don't invite us to a life of legalism and petty rule keeping. We are not supposed to end up weighed down with rules and regulations. We are invited, instead, to pattern our lives after the Teaching, the Torah, God gave to Moses. This is such a good and positive thing. That's why Jesus made it the pattern for His own teaching, and His guide in life.

When we build our lives on all sorts of other things and certainties, which might be here today and gone tomorrow, we are not in the best place, bearing in mind that God is our Judge (verses 4-5). When we take God's Torah teaching seriously, by contrast, we can flourish as He intends (verses 1-3). We feast on the Scriptures day and night, and we find this nourishes and refreshes us. We can then prosper in the things God gives us to do, because we're not relying on ourselves. We also become fruitful with something useful to share with others when it's required in life.

In some senses, this means that our thinking is supposed to be shaped by the Scriptures. We are then in a position to say something that is timely and wise as the need arises. This can be highly important to someone who is in a place of confusion, and really has no idea of the way ahead. At the best of times people don't need our ideas, suggestions and hunches. But they certainly do need to hear from God, especially when things are difficult for them. He really can use our godly thinking in this way when we delight in His Teaching. And delighting in His Word, we come to know ourselves to be truly blessed (verse 1). In a world like ours, this is a wonderful thing.

Let's Worship God
Read Psalm 100

This Psalm is such a great invitation to worship. On the one hand, it's a message to the whole earth; the universe should shout to the Lord with joy. He is the earth's Creator, after all. But more than that, we know that we are His flock, and that He, by extension, is our Shepherd. Even though the psalmist naturally considers the earth when He thinks of giving praise to God, there's another note he strikes.

The fact that God is to be worshipped at the Temple in Jerusalem is also significant in this song of praise. It is when praise is given in the

Temple courts that God is known to be good, loving, and motivated by His covenant faithfulness to the Children of Israel. That's a good thing. We really wouldn't want to worship a God who was one thing today and something else tomorrow. An unfaithful God is bad news all round.

I love what this Psalm says to us. We're worshipping God, and this is, rightly, something that is both personal and, in a way, private. But there's another emphasis that's important, too, and that's the Hebrew term "Tikkun Olam." This speaks to us about the healing of the world. As God's people, we are meant to care for the earth He has created and entrusted to us. Though we should never get to the point of making the earth our god and worshipping it, we do need to take care of it with absolute seriousness. Who knows, in caring for the world in the practical things we do, this might even be part of our witness to the Creator who is also our Saviour.

We join others in doing the right thing, ecologically, I mean. At the same time, we can also speak about our personal relationship with Him. The God who created others wants them to know Him as Saviour too. We think of the earth in the decisions we make. We also pray for people we know who wouldn't even claim that God was their Saviour. We pray that one day, that's just what they'll know Him to be. He's Creator, He's Saviour, and He's always worthy to receive our praise and worship.

God, the Active Player
Read Psalm 127

Throughout the Scriptures we find two ideas which could seem contradictory if pushed to unbiblical extremes. The one is the reality of human responsibility. This is seen when individuals pray, make sensible decisions in line with God's teaching, and then find blessing and success in His purposes. To the human eye, these characters are the active players.

There is another truth found in Scripture, however. This underlines that ultimately God is the active player. He decides, has the final word, and overrules on occasions that His will is done. As I say, if these are pushed to extremes, we end up with a whole lot of unhelpful living, based on a whole lot of unhelpful teaching.

It isn't intended in the Bible that we live like dead fish on a slab, doing nothing and deciding nothing. We would then end up praying that God would do something for us, but nothing seems to happen. Nothing materializes, and that's not surprising. We were never intended to be passive before our Creator. At the other extreme, it isn't intended either that we hurtle round the place making our own decisions without a thought for God; it's as if He'll take what He's given and ought to be happy with that.

Today's Psalm is wise, and in many ways helps us to get the balance right, when viewed in the light of the Scriptures as a whole. This one is from Solomon, one of Israel's greatest ever kings. He built the spectacular Temple in Jerusalem, something his father would have dearly loved to do, but was prevented by God. He also built up, and established, his family. He was a busy man, that's for sure. And yet, in this song of praise, we're told that God was really the One who underpinned all of this success.

If God isn't the true builder of the house, it never gets built, or continues to stand. The Temple certainly ended up built and completed on his watch. Also on Solomon's watch, the city of Jerusalem was perfectly safe, even bearing in mind that Israel had known her fair share of opponents and enemies. Alongside this, we also know that God built up his family life, his dynasty, if you will.

In a world in which a person's future security depended upon their family, this is so important, crucial in fact. Yes, Solomon built the Temple, and kept Jerusalem safe. All of this was possible because God kept him safe; his family would be safe and secure, because, ultimately, God was the active player. Though Solomon was a busy chap, as we mentioned before, all he achieved was built on God, and, in a real sense, built by God.

Certainly God has work for us to do, and things for us to achieve. These are sure to be accomplished when we play our part, yet recognize that He is the One that counts. What He builds ultimately stays built. And as we do what He asks of us, we can know that He is the One who holds us secure in the palm of His hand.

Our Glorious King

Read Psalm 24

This Psalm has a particular structure with three sections. The first (verses 1-2) makes certain statements about God, and the second (verses 3-6) gives observations about what kind of people we should be as His worshippers. The final section (verses 7-10) affirms that God is our glorious King.

In it, we find the idea that God is the One who rules over the whole world which He has established and made firm. He doesn't allow chaos to have the final word in things. In the light of this truth, His people can enter the Temple in assurance of His ultimate triumph in everything.

Once His people make their way into the Temple, they describe God accurately. He is the King of glory. And after worshipping Him they will return with a real blessing from the Lord. But this will only be the case when they have an intention to live properly before the King of glory. What this means is that if we understand God aright, we will want to have clean hands, a pure heart, and a truthful mouth which avoids speech which is false and deceitful.

Now, of course, this does mean making sure we don't go chasing off after false gods. We don't ignore all the teaching God gave to Moses and construct a god in our own image. We will need to speak truthfully about the one and only God. But we can't do that if we are happy to lie and say any old thing at other times, just because it may be to our short term benefit. We must be truthful people all the time, who do the right thing with clean hands. We will also want to have godly thoughts and affections. In brief, we will want to live a holy life before the King of glory. Nothing less could possibly be appropriate.

Is your life always perfectly holy and godly? Though I dearly want mine to be, it certainly isn't yet. I'm sure that if I claimed it already was, you would doubt that claim. You'd be right as well. I don't always do the right thing, think the right thing, or say the right thing. But I want to, I really do, as, I'm sure, you do.

As we place ourselves at the disposal of God, the King of glory, our life and our worship can eventually come more into harmony. We say the right thing about God in worship. And we do this from a life which is increasingly holy. The God who conquered the waters of chaos and established His earth (verse 2) is able to conquer our lack of holiness if we let Him. Then, because He is our Victor, He can create more godliness and holiness in you and me. He can make us the people He wants us to be. And that can't be a bad thing. Let's trust His ability to do just that.

Don't Be Unsettled By Those Who Do Wrong
Read Psalm 37:1-17

One thing I love about the Psalms is the way they describe life as it is. The bad bits aren't airbrushed out. The truth is that there are some people around who seem to commit themselves to wickedness. And, as far as we can tell, they don't appear to be any the worse for it, not in this world, anyway. The fact is that it seems all too possible to thumb our nose at God, to reject His teaching, and to get away with it in the here and now. Let's face it, this really can grate, certainly if God's teaching is precious to us.

The psalmist in today's reading seems to have been juggling with this kind of thinking as well. Jesus did too, come to think of it. We know this because He quoted from it in the Sermon on the Mount. He taught that the meek will inherit the land, as in the Land of Israel (Psalm 37:11; Matthew 5:5), the place God promised to His people. The Psalm tells us that the meek, or the lowly, will end up inheriting the land. They will be able to delight in all of the abundant well-being He gives. It might be true that those who ignore God can seem to be none the worse for their choice. But the truth is that it is those who take Him and His teaching seriously who ultimately inherit all the good things God has for them. That's the case in this world and in the world to come.

This wonderful Psalm is an acrostic. What that means is that verses in this song of praise begin systematically with each letter of the Hebrew alphabet in turn. As he writes it, it's almost as if the writer seems to have taken his eye off the ball, in a way. He's particularly obsessing about those who turn away from God and seem to get away with it. As he writes, however, he realises that God is calling him back to following His teaching. He is called to follow what God has said. If we want to do the right thing in the light of the Scriptures, we can leave the rest with God. When we fret and fuss in many ways, we put ourselves on God's throne, and wonder why He isn't doing a better job of sorting other people out. Returning to God, on our part, means that we end up knowing He will uphold us, and our cause. Why should we worry?

God can be relied upon to do the right thing at the right time. Verses 39-40 remind us that He is our salvation, and our protection. And we don't need to sort it out for ourselves, or sort them out, come to think of it. This is because He is the One who can be relied upon to help and deliver us. We can always trust Him to do this. He will, because He will always be true to His nature. We can depend upon that.

The Lord Reigns

Read Psalm 93

So, the Lord reigns. This is eternally true. Over the years, many have believed that this Psalm speaks about the Messiah, the One who will introduce the Messianic Age of blessing and peace. We are able to find real security in this, knowing that the Lord is our Rock. That means that there is nothing we need to fear, when we understand who He is.

Taking this insight seriously, we see today's passage describing life's difficulties and turbulence in the light of the Messianic Age which is to come. It's true, there are times when chaotic seas are much in evidence, and these great waves make a huge noise (verses 3-4). Yes, at times they can be rather frightening. When that's all kicking off, the rebellious nature of those who are against God and His anointed Messiah seems to drown out the voice of God. At least, it can seem like that in the short term. But we are reminded in these verses that there is another reality, another power, and He is mightier and stronger than anything we can see rebelling against Him at present.

The eternal God is strong. He will not allow the world of His creation to be overturned. He is on the throne, and no-one and nothing can depose Him. The Lord on high is mighty. This Psalm ends on an important note. The One who is victorious over every rebellion, and will be seen to be as well, is worshipped at the Temple in Jerusalem. God's Word is eternal, and He is to be worshipped always, regardless of how things might seem in the short term.

When things are tough, worshipping God is an act of faith. We might feel that things are hard, but when we give Him the praise He is due, we begin to see things in proportion once more. Let the waters pound. God is greater, mightier and more majestic than all of them. We live, and go on making appropriate decisions, in the light of His eternal reality.

The Shepherd, My Warrior
Read Psalm 23

When I was little, I remember seeing a particular picture of Jesus. This often tended to crop up on certificates given on the occasion of Infant Dedication, or when a baby was included on a church's Cradle Roll. The picture I'm thinking about is of Jesus the Shepherd. Invariably, He would look kind and pastoral, and He might have a little lamb in His arms. The message is clear: Jesus cares, even for me, even for the very young. Well, this is certainly true and helpful, as far as it goes. We need to cherish its message. But when we think about what Scripture says about shepherds, without contradicting the above picture of Jesus, there is much more to say.

In ancient Israel, and the world in which it was set, kings were sometimes thought of as shepherds. And, as with those who cared directly for flocks of sheep, shepherds were warriors. They had to be. They fought against predators and wild animals. They were prepared to shed the blood of those who wanted to damage, scatter and devour the flock. The well-being of the sheep was paramount. A shepherd wouldn't have been much use without this part of the job description. You can't simply ask a predator to play nice.

This truth is meant to be a comfort to us. Certainly this is underlined in today's Psalm. In it, God Himself is described as our Shepherd. When King David thought about His Lord's weapons, and His willingness to fight for him (verse 4), he drew comfort. Enemies who came against David were defeated and ultimately powerless to injure him (verse 5). Truly, the thought of God, our Warrior-Shepherd, fighting for us is quite remarkable. It's meant to be, because this is what happens when we are in a covenant relationship with a God like ours.

He is concerned about our safety. That will be one reason why the ministry of Nehemiah will have been so important. He knew God wanted him to rebuild the wall of Jerusalem so that the returning Exiles could be safe in their ancestral home. God is also interested in leading us into good and pleasant ways. When bad times come, and come they do, He wants to lead us through them, and out the other side into good times once more. In fact, He has a banquet prepared for us, in the presence of our defeated foes.

Some people these days would have us believe that God never gets involved in things in this world. He loves us, but stays out of the fray. There are also those who would like us to accept the view that good things are bad for us. Suffering is good for the soul, they say. It's as if God would never demean Himself by wanting us to enjoy the good things He has prepared for us. The truth is, however, that we find a very different and much more encouraging picture of God in the Scriptures in general, and in Psalm 23 in particular. He is our Shepherd, our Guide, our Warrior, and our Host who prepares lavish things for us. In the light of today's reading, it's important we don't trade-in the God of Scripture for a miserly, more hands-off kind of god. King David knew better than this, and so can we.

What a City, What a God

Read Psalm 122

Jerusalem dominates this Psalm, and in many ways it dominates the Scriptures, too. No other city comes close.

In some senses, the link between Jerusalem and Scripture begins way back in Genesis 22, when Abraham is told to travel to Moriah, a place that's associated with the later location of that most important town. There he and his son will worship and offer sacrifice. Again in the first five books of the Bible, we read that God chooses to be worshipped in Jerusalem, and that His people must travel there to celebrate Passover, Pentecost and Tabernacles at the Temple. In other books in Scripture, we are told about the Kings of Judah who resided there. And there are countless mentions of the place in the writings of the Prophets. That's certainly true of the Psalms and other writings in which we read of the rebuilding of the city, its walls and of the Temple after the Exile. Jerusalem features heavily in the Gospels and other writings of the early followers of Jesus, too. And, indeed, in Revelation, heavenly worship is linked with the New Jerusalem. So, from beginning to end, Scripture takes this place most seriously.

In today's song of praise, the worshipper is obviously excited to be there, and to be able to worship God properly. That comes through so clearly. What a wonderful place it is. It's the place of worship and justice. In addition to that, it is there that His people will pray. Then they will know the city to be a place of peace.

It is quite understandable that we, like the psalmist, become attached to worship, and to all that we know is precious about it. Nothing really comes close in this world to the joy of worshipping the Lord, and standing in His presence. I'm sure that, like me, you can think of times when you have been aware of the heaviness of the presence of God. This is much more than the sum total of all that we say, pray and sing in church. God is with us as we worship, not only because He says He will be whenever He is praised, but also because He wants us to experience something of His imminence. It isn't that the crowd is being "worked." Rather, the Sovereign God is drawing close to His children.

Now, of course, we shouldn't chase after such experiences. The spiritually counterfeit can produce experiences, too. Worship is about what He deserves to receive, not about how we feel. But when we genuinely focus on Him, and praise Him in the best way we know how, let's not be surprised if He simply draws close in an intimate and wonderful way. Our God is a most wonderful God after all. And He wouldn't want to keep His distance from us. Jesus coming into the world is ample demonstration of that.

Calling Upon God
Read Psalm 91

Over the years, I've probably thought that each Psalm, in turn, is my favourite one. There's a great deal of amazing teaching and practical wisdom for living found in them. The fact is, that I've been particularly attached to today's Psalm when life's been difficult and I've needed to turn to God for help. It's such a gem. The psalmist who is praying it has been through massive difficulty. But he has come to know the Lord's help and encouragement. In turn, he, then, encourages others to trust God as he has done.

We find, here, such a reassuring picture of God extending His wings over us. How wonderful it is to find that we can rest secure under the protection He gives. The Psalmist isn't being simplistic, of course. He knows that there are many arrows and snares in life. We can have enemies after all. But this isn't a Psalm in which the one who prays exclusively focusses on himself. No, he's focussing on God, his fortress, the One in whom he really can trust.

These verses move forward step by step until they end with an affirmation that when we look to God, we will certainly be shown His salvation. Truth to tell, when we understand this, we know that salvation isn't simply something we experience on the other side of death, in His nearer presence. We experience something of it in the here and now as well.

The psalmist was obviously a person with a testimony of the goodness of God, who saves and rescues us. I'm sure we also have testimonies of our own. When we rehearse them – these stories of God's victory in our lives – we strengthen our faith in Him. As time goes on, He becomes more and more important, and the sound and fury of our attackers recede. So, let's call on Him. He will be sure to answer.

How Lovely is God's Dwelling-Place
Read Psalm 84

Even one day in the Temple courts is better than a thousand anywhere else. That's the view of the worshipper who gave us this song of praise. He'd rather express his humility with God's people than be "in" with those who have other priorities (verses 10-11). That shows character.

Here in Psalm 84, there's the kind of emphasis on God and the loveliness of the place of worship that we would expect with one of the Songs of Zion (verses 5 and 7). What we also find, here, is a description of the positive difference all of this makes to life day by day. The psalmist knows he's going to need to travel through dry and difficult places sometime or other (verse 6). Yet, in all of the scorching heat and dryness, he knows that he can look to God and trust in Him.

But rain isn't guaranteed to arrive on cue, not even in Israel. We know that there were times of famine and absence of rain (1 Kings 18:2). For the writer of this Psalm, though, after a long, hot, summer and a long, hot, climb all the way up to Jerusalem, he was still looking to God. There's nothing simplistic going on, here. He simply keeps on trusting the Lord. And he's determined to get to the place of worship, come what may.

The psalmist is still convinced, through the long, hard, trudge that God is good, and he wants good and positive things for him as well. He wants his own walk to be blameless, of course, and he knows God wants to show him favour and honour (verse 11). One reason why he knows this, is because he can see one of God's blessings standing before him at the Temple, because God gave the people their king, the one who would fight for them and protect them. God has blessed one way, so He can be trusted to bless in other ways as well.

When we look at our lives, what blessings do we see? I'm sure we'll notice all sorts of good things which have God's finger-prints on, so to speak. In the light of these, and more importantly in the light of His Word, we can go on trusting Him, however dry and difficult things might be at the moment. He has never let us down before. He isn't going to start now. How could He?

Flourishing Like a Palm-Tree
Read Psalm 92

I remember staying in West Jerusalem one December a number of years ago. I was on sabbatical from ministry and had planned my time well. January would see a return to the pattern of ministry that was normal for me. I was determined to use this three month period wisely, as it could only occur once during my ministry. Anyway, during my four weeks in Jerusalem – a city I love a great deal – the temperature was unseasonably extremely hot. Then, over one weekend, there was torrential rain, not to mention very high winds.

The picture that will stay with me was what I saw on venturing out from the small hotel in which I was staying once the storm was over. It was just at the top of Ben Yehuda Street. Frankly, I couldn't believe my eyes. All around the place, a whole variety of trees had been snapped off like twigs. These large tree trunks were now left lying in the road, or propped up against things just where they fell.

One tree that seems to fare well during such storms is the palm-tree. These tend not to get snapped off like other trees. I've heard it suggested that during storms palm-trees might be blown almost horizontal. At the end of the high winds, however, they're still going to be there, and standing tall once more, when other more apparently sturdy trees are lying in the street.

I love the fact that in Psalm 92 there's a promise God gives in verse 12. This tells us that we need to live rightly before Him. In turn, He wants to see us flourishing, like a palm-tree in the Temple. His invitation to us is to be fruitful throughout life and into old age. We might have faced all sorts of storms and difficulties over the years. If we really are rooted in Him, however, He'll see to it that though we might be bowed down from time to time, we won't be broken. This really is such a lovely picture of the child of God who wants to serve Him and be fruitful in His work.

Others – "the wicked" - seem to flourish in the short term (verse 7), but they will not stand eternally before God. We'll remember that this was the message of Psalm 1. If we want to prosper (Psalm 1:3), we really do need to delight in Him and His teaching. There are no short cuts, here. When we are rooted in Him, certain things follow. When we choose not to take Him seriously, again certain other things follow. Jesus understood this, and taught it clearly in His parable about the two builders (Matthew 7:24-27). Both houses faced similar storms, but the one built on the foundation of His teaching, survived. The other one didn't. It isn't about getting lucky, it's about getting rooted.

Let's continue to be rooted in Him. He really does want us to stand tall, with roots that go down deep into His Word. Whatever comes, with His help we'll be equal to the challenge.

JESUS, GLORY AND BELIEF – THE FIRST THREE SIGNS IN JOHN'S GOSPEL

Be Guided By Jesus

Read John 2:1-5

How easy it is to get an idea then go hurtling off in that direction. Let's face it, we've all done it from time to time and have the T-shirt. Sometimes, it is likely to result in embarrassment. Truth to tell, anyone who tries to counsel us not go there or to do it might get crushed as we rush past them. Impetuosity means we just won't listen, we won't take telling. In such a mode, we're quite unteachable and unreachable. But wisdom means that we're prepared to admit that we're not the fount of all knowledge, and that God's perspective is greater than ours. This really seems to have been a lesson the mother of Jesus had already learnt.

In today's reading, we find Jesus, His mother, and His rabbinic disciples, at a wedding in Cana in Galilee, not all that far away from Nazareth. The meal was probably over by this point, because the practice of handwashing before eating had already taken place. We know this because the large water jars were empty. The mother of Jesus noticed there was a problem, however. Significantly, John refers to her in such a respectful way (verse 1), because by the time he wrote this Gospel, she was, in effect, his mother too (John 19:26-27).

She immediately goes to Jesus with the problem and explains to Him that the supply of wine had given out. Perhaps she expected Him to do something about it. According to one translation He refers to her respectfully as "Mother" (The Complete Jewish Bible). Jesus explains that He shouldn't necessarily do anything about this at all. This is because His time hasn't yet come. He knows that in the future, however, His hour will come both to perform miraculous signs, and to suffer a grim Roman execution for our sins. But, for the moment, He initially seems to want to step back from the problem.

By the time this incident had come to a close with the verses we'll read tomorrow, Jesus had changed His mind. Why, we don't know. But for now, the mother of Jesus leaves the matter with Him. She simply speaks to the servants and tells them to do whatever He says. This is so wise.

When something significant is going on, and we know there's a problem, we may need to do what we think is appropriate. That being said, however, we will always need to listen to godly advice, and to leave the matter with the Lord. Whatever He eventually decides to do about things is up to Him not us. Wisdom sometimes counsels us not to blunder in and make the matter worse, just because we've got an idea. It's always good to remind ourselves who's on the throne. From there, His perspective is greater than ours.

Jesus' Limitless Resources
Read John 2:6-11

There's nothing worse than running on empty. There isn't garage for miles around, and we're not even sure we'll be able to make it to the destination. To make matters worse, there's no phone signal and we can't even let others know we're going to be late. It can be something like this when we're too busy for too long, and we don't take care to top up our spiritual resources. We look at the diary and wonder how on earth we'll get through the coming week. Perhaps, in various ways, we've all been there.

Certainly the family of the young bridegroom in today's reading were at the end of their natural resources in a big way. Out of what they had they'd adequately provided for the wedding meal itself. But they hadn't been able to provide enough wine for the guests. This would have been highly embarrassing and very public. It's like us taking everyone out for a big meal, only for our credit cards to get rejected when we try to settle the bill. We don't really know why Jesus seems to have changed His mind about all of this. In yesterday's reading He seems to think it isn't necessarily His place to get involved, because His time hadn't yet come. But by the verses we're looking at today He's obviously fully involved. Did He see the family's distress and shame and have compassion for them? We really don't know.

The servants follow Jesus' direction. They fill the six large stone jars with water. Some gets drawn out and taken to the person who's in charge of the celebrations. But now he's amazed at the family's generosity and resources. Unlike everyone else, they've keep the very best wine for this point in the proceedings. How generous they are, what a wonderful family. That's the practical difference Jesus makes. His resources, unlike ours, are limitless. What John narrates, here, is the first miraculous sign Jesus performs. He describes seven of them between the beginning of chapter 2 and the end of chapter 12.

By the time John completes his Gospel, he knows that it is Jesus who really is the Bridegroom of all who love Him. He'll write about this in chapter 14:1-4. And he'll drive this home in Revelation 19:9 when he refers to the wedding feast of the Lamb. The Lamb refers to Jesus Himself, and to His perfect sacrifice for sin. The verses we read today speak to us about His limitless resources. That's why it's so important that we spend time with Him each day. And as we do, we'll become increasingly thrilled that the One we love will provide a heavenly banquet for us. It couldn't get better than this.

Cleaning House
Read John 2:12-17

Having been brought up in Nazareth, the Rabbi from Galilee seems to have made Capernaum His base of operation. However, after a few days there, it was time for Jesus to go back up to Jerusalem to celebrate one of the Biblical feasts at the Temple. We are told in Leviticus 23 that all who were able should make their way to the Temple to celebrate Passover, Pentecost and Tabernacles (in Hebrew: Pesach, Shavuot and Sukkot). This time, it was the Passover that was approaching. And, as He journeyed there with His rabbinic disciples, He knew exactly what He'd find there at the Temple.

What He found there was something that looked like a veritable hub for commerce. Animals were sold for the required sacrifices. In addition to this, Roman currency was exchanged for Judean Temple coinage. As we've mentioned, it certainly wasn't the first time Jesus will have seen all of this. He will have been to the Temple a number of times a year, every year. This time, however, he decided that a response needed to be made. So, He took cords, made a whip out of them, and drove out all who bought and sold there. The Temple was meant to be His "Father's house." Now it has been turned into a hub of commerce.

In effect, in today's reading the "Son of God" (John 1:34) was reclaiming the Temple for His Father. Jesus wasn't cursing the place or indicating that He hated it and everything about it. Far from it. Indeed, the Temple continued to be the venue He chose in order to teach the people. What He was doing in today's verses was making it fit for His Father's ongoing purpose once more. The truth is that when the people of God respond to God, if we're not too careful, the resulting spiritual machinery can become an end in itself. People get processed by it, and God gets what He's given. Secondary things should never dethrone the One who should always be our primary concern.

Are we getting weighed down by the many spiritual and religious things we've convinced ourselves God demands from us? We really can. Have we convinced ourselves that He will be angry if we don't read 28 chapters of the Bible before breakfast? Will He really want to squash us like a bug if we ever take time off to listen to music, pamper ourselves at the spa, go out for a coffee, or spend quality time with our family? If we are too harsh with ourselves for too long, we can end up with that kind of picture of God. And where's the joy in that? Let's clean away all of the unnecessary things that take the joy out of our experience of the Lord. Let's clean house and remove the things He has never demanded of us, but we have been demanding of ourselves and others. He longs to spend quality time with us. It's important that we don't lose that joy and delight.

Hero and Zero
Read John 2:18-25

Whatever our age, we've probably already noticed by now that not everyone loves us. Some? Yes, absolutely. Others? Not so much. For some, we might be something approaching a hero. For others, we're more like a zero, we're counted as nothing at all. How we respond to those who are not our greatest admirers can say an awful lot about us, however. That's certainly the case for Jesus, too.

As we think of the four Gospels, the vast majority of those who believed in Jesus, loved His teaching, and followed Him, were members of the Jewish community in which He lived. Most of these, including His rabbinic disciples, were from Galilee in the north of the Land of Israel (in Hebrew, Eretz Israel). He seemed to have some supporters further south in Judea as well. When we think of people from the south who were for Him, a number of people come to mind. There'll be the person who leant Jesus the donkey on which He rode into Jerusalem, and the person who allowed Him to use his upper room, so that He could celebrate the Passover with His disciples just before He was handed over to the authorities. Then there'll be religious leaders, part of the Judean establishment, like Nicodemus, and Joseph of Arimathea. All of these are decendents of Abraham, Isaac and Jacob too. Verse 23 refers to some of these as well.

There were other members of the Judean religious establishments, it must be said, who took a very different view. They thought Jesus was challenging their authority, and, therefore, the authority of the Roman Emperor. The reason for this is that the Chief Priest, who stood at the centre of the Judean establishment, was appointed by Caesar, and was part politician, and part religious leader. His job was to keep the lid on things and to make sure that good order was always maintained. From the Chief Priest's point of view, with Jesus around, there could easily be trouble, and the troops might need to be called to restore order. The

Chief Priest would always need to be guided by the dominant thought WWCD, What Would Caesar Do?

These religious officials are referred to in verse 20. Now, in a way, it might be better to think of them as "Judeans" rather than "Jews" because, as we've said, Jesus and the overwhelming majority of His followers were members of the Jewish community as well. Jesus, however, seemed not to be prepared to jump through hoops for those who questioned His authority. In verse 19. Jesus made it clear to them that once His Heavenly Father had raised Him from the dead on the third day, that would be answer enough for them. In the meantime, He could leave His cause in His Father's hands. They might take Him to be hero or zero, but His reputation and future were safe with God.

Now, courtesy is always a good thing, that's true enough. But jumping through hoops for those who have malice towards us is rarely a productive thing to do. If we are being wronged or unhelpfully challenged, whatever the right response happens to be, we are always in a good place when we allow our Heavenly Father to fight for us. Let's face it, He's a far better vindicator for us than we could ever be.

Two Rabbis and the Spirit of God
Read John 3:1-15.

Overhearing what's yelled during a bar fight is one thing. Being invited into the company of two very learned rabbis as they discuss important and difficult things is rather different. John invites us to do just that in chapter 3 of his Gospel, to listen to two rabbis, I mean.

A rabbi from Judea in the south of the country has privately come to see a Rabbi from Galilee in the north. They obviously understand a great deal about the Scriptures they love, but the concepts these Scriptures describe are not always easy to understand, however learned you might be. How can it ever be possible to fully understand the Spirit of God? Things in Scripture certainly can be difficult, even for the wisest and the cleverest.

For example, there's the teaching Moses gave in Genesis 1:2 about the role of the Spirit in Creation. The Spirit is referred to there with the Hebrew word Ruah, and this can mean spirit, wind or breath, not easy concepts to pin down. When Genesis was translated into Greek a couple of hundred years before this conversation in chapter 3 took place, the word Pneuma was used in place of the word Ruah. That's the word John uses here as he relates the exchange between these two learned rabbis.

The Rabbi from Galilee is inviting His rabbinic colleague to experience something rather special. It's as if Jesus is inviting Nicodemus to experience, first hand, what was taught by the Prophet Ezekiel centuries before (Ezekiel 36:25-27). Ezekiel taught the people of God about the possibility of being washed clean from sin, being given a new heart, and receiving the Spirit of God deep within.

Jesus described this as being "born again" or "born from above" using the Greek word "Anothen." But again, all of this is so difficult to pin down. Nicodemus was a good and able man. But sometimes, even when we are good and able, it can be so difficult to admit our spiritual need. This is so especially if in many ways we are people of experience and are used to teaching or helping others. For the spiritually mature who teach, it can be hard when the boot's on the other foot, so to speak. We know that Nicodemus was a mature and humble person, because, by the time John's Gospel comes to an end, he seems to have received precisely what Jesus offered him, here. He didn't storm off in high dudgeon as more brittle people sometimes do.

Do we need to know the reality of being born again by the Spirit of God? Perhaps we have spent much time around those who obviously have experienced this for themselves. Even if we have lived in Christian circles, the truth is that it's still possible for us not to have experienced this at all. Now, of course, there's no time like the present. Knowing about spiritual rebirth, and receiving it, are two very different things. Only the second of the two can transform our life. When we commit to Jesus, and confess our sins to our Heavenly Father, however, we really can know what it is to receive this new birth in all its fullness. And if we already do know this for ourselves, we still have the privilege of opening our heart to God day by day so that we can go on being filled by God Himself. What a wonderful thing this is. Wherever we are in life, we can have a transformational encounter with Him today.

Two Rabbis and Eternal Life
Read John 3:16-21

Sometimes, little ones admit to being afraid of the dark. All sorts of dangers are imagined to lurk in the shadows, though in reality they don't. In this fertile soil, fear can grow unchecked. Many years ago I heard unnecessary fear being described by the acronym F.E.A.R. - False Expectations that Appear Real. Fear, even unfounded fear, really can be so crippling.

In yesterday's reading, the Judean rabbi had come to see Jesus by night. What Jesus wanted for him was to live in the spiritual light that God had made available. Both rabbis knew that on the other side of death lay two very different outcomes. The Scriptures of ancient Israel made this plain in Daniel 12:2. This taught that following death, some would be resurrected for eternal life, and others would be resurrected for something less heavenly. Jesus wanted Nicodemus to know what it was to go on living a righteous life, and to be assured that not even death could separate him from God's light. In Him, there was nothing at all to fear.

As believers, we are supposed to know that nothing, not even death, can separate us from the love of God. Jesus' great follower Paul wrote about this in his Letter to the Romans, in chapter 8 verses 38-39. Paul certainly knew that having accepted Jesus, the Messiah of Israel, life stretched out before him, and presented so many opportunities for him to express his gratitude to God. He explains this in another letter, the Letter to the Ephesians. Here he writes that he had already experienced salvation through the grace of God. Life now opened the door to concrete ways in which he could be good and kind to others (Ephesians 2:8-10). These were the kind of good deeds for which he had been saved.

It's great to know that we have eternal life. It really is good to know that nothing can ever separate us from the Lord, and that we have nothing to fear. By the same token, it's also good to recognize the needs of others, and to see in people around us an opportunity to express the love of God in practical and down to earth ways. A mature and holy life informs us that other people matter to God too. I wonder, how can we help others today?

Spiritual Washing
Read John 3:22-26

2,000 years ago in the Jewish community, spiritual washing was important as a way of indicating a desire to take God seriously. If people from other communities wanted to become part of the Children of Israel, they would be totally immersed in running water, or living water. This indicated that their new life was important to them, and they wanted to take the nature of the Holy One of Israel seriously too. A community lived together on the shores of the Dead Sea, because of their desire to live a holy life. If a person joined them, again they would also need to be spiritually washed by being totally immersed in water.

Both Jesus and His cousin John – sometimes referred to as John the Baptist – called people to turn to God, and take Him particularly seriously. That's what they preached. Just to say that this person John isn't the one who wrote the Gospel we're reading at the moment. That was John, the brother of James, who was one of Jesus' rabbinic disciples. Anyway, in today's reading, we are told about the importance of spiritual washing in the ministries of Jesus and John the Baptist.

John was immersing people at a place called Aenon. Jesus and His rabbinic disciples were in the Judean wilderness immersing people as well. We read that a debate occurred, about the whole matter of spiritual washing, between some of John's disciples and an unnamed Judean. Some of these disciples went to their rabbi, John, and drew his attention to the fact that an increasing number of people were being washed by Jesus and His disciples. In tomorrow's verses we'll have an opportunity to think together about the humility of John's response to this observation.

Perhaps today we could reflect for a few moments about the importance of taking God seriously, and wanting to share in His holy nature. Of course, those who came to Jesus and His cousin John, and responded positively to their message, were already members of the people of God. But they still needed to renew their commitment to Him. The effect of that, for them, would have been so important and life-changing.

We might know that we've been believers for many years. That's a good thing. It can be of crucial importance, however, to rekindle the spiritual flame in our heart. Otherwise we can simply "coast" into the future with a sense that what we're giving to God is enough. The writer of this Gospel also spoke about the importance of not losing our first love for Jesus (Revelation 2:4). It can be so easy for that kind of thing to happen, even if we don't intend it to. Perhaps as we take our reading of the Scriptures, and our heartfelt worship of God, with the seriousness they deserve, we can make sure this doesn't happen to us. And if we recognize that it already has, God would be so thrilled to welcome us back. Even today. Our first love for Him can be renewed and refreshed.

It's Not All About Me
Read John 3:27-36

Now, of course, it depends upon how we're wired. Sometimes, truth to tell, we can end up thinking that it's all about us. Why wouldn't it be? Others might be crashing and burning all around, but we're the ones that matter. The more successful we are, the easier it can be to succumb to this kind of wrong thinking. How easy it could have been for Jesus' cousin John (the Baptist) to think it was all about him.

This certainly could have been the case, because, by any standards, John had a successful ministry. People were seeking him out, and he was causing quite a stir, or splash, if you prefer. It even looks possible from the text that a religious scholar from Judea sought him out to discuss important things. John's humility and mature character meant that when his own disciples told him about the popularity of Jesus, he was more than happy to point away from himself. John describes himself like being the friend of the bridegroom, or like Elijah who announces the arrival of the long-awaited Messiah. When we're at home in our own skin and inwardly at peace, we know that others can shine around us without it being a personal affront. If we were to learn the lesson of what John modelled for us, how many squabbles in families, churches and other organizations could be prevented?

John was genuinely happy with the ministry our Heavenly Father had given him. He would get to play such an important role in God renewing His covenant with the House of Israel and the House of Judah, something about which the Prophet Jeremiah had taught (31:31-37). God's relationship with His people would become even more intimate because of the ministry of his cousin Jesus, and John was thrilled at the role he himself got to play.

Do we need God to minister to us so that we don't get easily undermined, and unnecessarily threatened by others? He certainly will if we let Him. Even if others eclipse us, we can still shine with God's light. And knowing that it's not all about us, we also have the privilege of being a real encouragement to others. Part of our ministry today might be to message someone and thank them for the good things they're doing, even if others haven't noticed their excellent work. Or again, we might get the chance of emailing someone who's unfairly going through the wringer. Is God asking us to encourage someone? Our encouragement can make such a difference to them, and it will indicate before God that we know it isn't all about us.

Reaching Out

Read John 4:1-15

A number of years ago, if someone wanted to do something really imaginative, and reach out to a person who was very different from themselves, they might have needed to travel some distance in order to do it. We hear about missionaries who did this, people like Gladys Aylward and William Carey. They took courageous decisions to reach people they wouldn't normally have met. Gladys Aylward left the UK for China in the early 20th Century, and the Baptist missionary William Carey set sail for India towards the end of the 18th Century.

In our days, if we want to reach out to others, people with whom we usually wouldn't socialize, we won't always need to travel far at all. Partly that's because folk from other parts of the world now enrich us by being part of the vibrant and very diverse life of the UK. In addition to this, these days society is so tribal. It's easy for many of us to live in our own bubbles. We can easily choose to socialize only with people like us, people who agree with us on the great issues of the day. An extreme form of this encourages us to think that people whose views differ from ours must truly be vile and immoral. If they weren't, surely they'd agree with us. They need to be shut down. They need to be prevented from contributing to society. And round and round we go. But we can leave the seductive safety of our own social echo-chambers quite easily, if we have a mind to do so. We can reach out.

In today's reading, Jesus chose to reach out as well. He needed to travel from Judea in the south of Israel to Galilee in the north. He made an unusual decision to take the direct route, but this took Him right through some pretty hostile territory. He belonged to descendants of Abraham, Isaac and Jacob who had a high view of the Temple in Jerusalem, which is why He chose to worship there so often. In today's reading He met a woman who was a Samaritan. The relationship between Jesus' community and the Samaritans was complex, difficult and sometimes violent. Samaritans also saw themselves as descendants of Abraham, Isaac and Jacob. The woman in these verses and Jesus had this in common. But Samaritans wanted nothing to do with Jerusalem, its leaders or its Temple. As a result, the community of which Jesus was a part tended to regard their Samaritan estranged relatives with a massive dose of suspicion.

In verse 7, Jesus asked this lady at the well for water to drink. In verse 10 He offered her living water. The Messiah asked the woman for her help, and then He offered her spiritual renewal and refreshment, things that only He could give.

In order for that to happen, however, Jesus took the decision to reach out to someone He could quite naturally have avoided. Are there people we are happy to avoid? Being human and sinful, we can all answer "Yes" to that. I wonder how the Lord would surprise us and bless us if we decided to reach out to someone else in a similar way. For you and me, this might mean simply speaking to someone we tend to avoid at work. It could mean chatting with particular courtesy to someone who is obviously different from us when they serve us in a café or a shop. Little acts of kindness can have positive results if we follow the prompting of God. Such encounters can also bring unexpected joy, to the other person and to us.

Truth Comes Calling
Read John 4:16-26

How wonderful it is that God, who knows everything about us, loves us and has forgiven us in Jesus His Son. That God knows us completely is one thing. We might be less happy if other people knew us as completely. There are some things about us that we are happy that no one else knows.

That would have been the case with the woman with whom Jesus was having a conversation in today's reading. Prophet that He was, the Rabbi from Galilee knew everything there was to know about this lady's domestic situation. In these verses, truth came calling for her in a big way. The instruction He gave her seemed innocuous enough: "Go call your husband." For a woman who had been married five times and was not married to her current partner, this presented something of a problem, it must be said.

What Jesus wanted for her more than anything else wasn't to embarrass her. It was to lead her to the point of knowing Him, the Messiah. In order to do this, however, He needed first of all to lead her from the point of estrangement from God and His purposes to the place of openness towards Him.

We mentioned yesterday that the relationship between Jesus' community and hers was complicated, though both groups were descendants of Abraham, Isaac and Jacob. Jesus' community worshipped at the Temple in Jerusalem. The lady's worshipped on Mount Gerizim near where this conversation was taking place, some 40 or so miles north of Jerusalem. They were certainly estranged, but they were related, too.

The woman with whom Jesus was talking was in serious danger of getting bogged down in all of the minutiae of estrangement. Jesus cuts through all of that. He tells her that salvation comes from His community, which rightly had a high view of the Temple in Jerusalem. Jesus doesn't tell her that the Samaritans' self-imposed separation from the Temple didn't matter. He did reach out to her, however, and invite her to have a renewed and restored relationship with our Heavenly Father through Himself, Israel's Messiah. This she does. His response to us is also the same, when we are estranged from Him in some way. He draws us into His love and eternal purposes, and asks us to bring Him our sin and brokenness. Then He can forgive us and heal us from our self-inflicted wounds.

Before concluding our reflection on today's passage, we can note two further things. The first is about the social relationship between men and women in Jesus' community 2,000 years ago. In verse 27, the rabbinic disciples of Jesus register surprise at their Rabbi's conversation with the lady in question. We need to take this at face value, of course. But we don't know exactly what triggered their surprise. Such conversations weren't at all unknown in the Jewish community 2,000 years ago.

The second matter is that of worshipping God in spirit and in truth, mentioned in verse 24. It isn't that Jesus despised the Temple, thought that worshipping there was unimportant, and going there was a bit of a chore. His own practice pointed clearly in the opposite direction, as He travelled there each year to celebrate Passover, Pentecost and Tabernacles. The point was this. By the time John completes his Gospel towards the end of the First Century CE, the Romans will have utterly destroyed the Temple some 20 or so years before. John records these words of Jesus for encouragement for believers in his own day. They may not be able to worship at the Temple ever again, but they can genuinely worship God in spirit and in truth. This is in line with the teaching God gave His people through Moses in the Books of Genesis to Deuteronomy. The guidance God gave through Moses never encouraged legalism, or doing things for Him on autopilot. He wants a relationship with us at heart level. He also wants to forgive and restore us, whatever skeletons we might have been keeping under lock and key. True spiritual worship was available for the woman in this story, and it is for us. It's important that we never allow the devil to rub our nose in something God has already forgiven. As someone once said: "When the devil wants to remind us about our past, remind him about his future."

Leading Others to Jesus
Read John 4:27-42

The woman of whom we read in chapter 4 of this Gospel clearly came to recognize Jesus as Messiah and Saviour. As we see today, following a particular exchange with the Rabbi, she left her water jar where it was at the well. She knew that He had spoken to her as a Prophet, and had made clear to her that He knew all about her. This, however, was good news not bad news. The lady went back to her village and shared what she was coming to know about Jesus. She posed the question to them as to whether or not He might be the Messiah.

Because of her testimony, many of the villagers not only came to see Jesus, they also came to faith in Him. What a big step this was for them, as we saw yesterday. This was due to the fact that this particular Rabbi was from Galilee, and His keeping of the Biblical feasts took Him three times a year to the Temple in Jerusalem, a place they despised with a passion. In coming to faith in Him, they were overcoming their estrangement from, and hostility to, these descendants of Abraham, Isaac and Jacob whom they hated with some enthusiasm. Jesus, with His love for the Temple and the writings of the Prophets, was the Messiah and the Saviour of the world. Their Father in Heaven, the Holy One of Israel, was both the Creator of the world, and the Saviour of the world. At one and the same time, He would always have special affection for Jerusalem, and His love for the whole of the world brought Jesus into it to die as a sacrifice for sin (3:16).

We notice that the woman in question didn't leave her water jar at the well, then go home and give a Biblical lecture lasting two and a half hours. She invited them to come and see. She also posed the question, "could this be…?" She ignited their understandable curiosity as to whether this Rabbi might be the long-awaited Messiah. She also invited them to do something which they could easily do, namely accompany her to see Him. She didn't manipulate them. She didn't work the crowd. She didn't lead them through a sales pitch ending with a clincher, by which time she knew she'd got 'em. She simply asked the question, Could this be…? This was followed by the invitation, Come and see. God could be trusted to save them Himself, and "close the deal," so to speak.

There's no greater privilege in life than leading someone to Jesus. Sometimes we can fail to do this because we imagine we have to set up the entire process for an individual, and guide them skilfully all the way through it, ourselves, from beginning to end. The truth is that our role in someone's conversion might be a simple conversation somewhere in the middle of the very long process which ends with saving faith. A dozen might have made a contribution before us. Two dozen might make a contribution after us. We don't always have to try to manage God – He knows what He's doing, after all. It is important, having said all of that, for us to play our part. If this amounts to speaking the words "Could this be…? Come and see" let's play our part faithfully, like the woman in today's reading. There isn't a believer anywhere on planet earth who can't do that.

The Word of Healing

Read John 4:43-54

Jesus has now arrived back in Galilee. He's in Cana, where He performed His first miraculous sign at a wedding. In today's passage He performs His second. He was welcomed ecstatically by the locals, descendants of Abraham, Isaac and Jacob one and all. They had been at the Temple in Jerusalem with Jesus celebrating the Passover. John now tells us that the Rabbi is approached by an official who worked for King Herod Antipas. The official's son lay sick back at home in Capernaum, some 15 or 16 miles away. Having heard that Jesus had finally made it to Galilee from Judea, he approached Him, for his son was at the point of death.

The assumption and request of the official, that Jesus should accompany him to Capernaum, were reasonable enough, it has to be said. Instead, Jesus asks him to exercise faith, and take Him at His word. The Rabbi informs the official that he can go home. When he gets there, he'll find his son quite recovered. The key phrase in this section is found in verse 50. This tells us that the official took Jesus at His word, and he acted on it. And, indeed, even before he reached his home, good news reached him. Servants told him of his son's recovery, and that this had happened the very moment Jesus spoke the word of healing.

What we read in all of this shows that Jesus is very much at home on the landscape inhabited by the Jewish community 2,000 years ago. This incident finds its pre-echoes in healings that prophets had performed centuries before. What's also happening here is that this official, probably not Jewish himself, joins the many descendants of Abraham in believing in Jesus.

Are there things with which we are grappling at the moment? It could be a health issue, or something more financial. It could be something in our own life. Indeed, it could be something happening to one of our loved ones, as was the case with this official. Whatever it is, we need to trust Jesus and have faith in His word. God sees the big picture, and will answer us, not in line with our ability to pray or to understand, but in line with His limitless love. When we trust, we are able to walk with Him through the dark and difficult times we face (Psalm 23:4). He can then lead us into places in which we are able to experience His joy once more. When we trust in Him, we are never disappointed.

Jesus Banishes Unbelief
Read John 5:1-9

If we only ever think that bad things can happen to us, this will shape so many of the things we say, and our decision-making. It can easily become a self-fulfilling prophecy of doom and gloom for us. Opportunities will be refused, and positive things will not be embraced. Unbelief reigns. Here in the third miraculous sign Jesus performs in John's Gospel, the Rabbi cuts through such unbelief, turns a man's life upside down, and gives him more than he ever expected. He had been lying on a mat day in day out for 38 years, along with others who were ill. He was convinced, however, that nothing in his situation could ever change. Others could be helped, but he never could.

Jesus is back in Jerusalem in Judea once more to celebrate another Biblical feast at the Temple. He is in Bethzatha in the city near the pool called Bethesda. This pool was surrounded by a walk-way with five covered colonnades. The area around the pool was a place for disabled people to gather. The reason for this was that it was believed that the occasional stirring of the water in the pool was caused by an angel; and the first person into the water after this happened would be healed.

The man's problem was that regardless of any angelic activity, because he didn't have anyone to help him into the pool, he was never going to get healed. His life was an endless round of begging from pilgrims who were in town to worship at the Temple. Jesus cut through his unbelief, spoke healing to him, and told him to pick up his mat and go home. But there was a problem.

This was a public area, and it was the Sabbath. Certainly when the incident took place, many in the Judean religious establishment regarded this as prohibited. But this might not have been the view of members of the Jewish community in Galilee, further north. The Rabbi from Galilee might easily have been simply practising what people there believed about how to celebrate the Sabbath.

We'll pick this up again in tomorrow's reading. Just to say, here, that Jesus effected a healing for the man which he didn't expect. The Lord had compassion for him, and enough faith for both of them. It's important that we allow Him to increase our vision, too. In many ways, the man's expectations were eminently sensible, bearing in mind that he didn't have anyone with him to help him into the pool. Being sensible, practical and wise is, of course, important. The opposite are hardly virtues that we should embrace with any regularity. Sometimes, however, what God wants for us is greater than we ever think is possible.

Perhaps no-one in our family has ever been to University; that isn't to say that we never could. No-one in our friendship circle may ever have written a book. We might not be able to think of any friend or relative who has recorded an album regardless of how much musical talent they undoubtedly have. None of our friends might have started a business. It's possible, just possible, that what God wants us to do might be something of a first for our friends and family. If God is asking us to follow a particular path, and this is confirmed by the advice of wise and godly friends, who says we can't achieve something quite remarkable? And let's not forget, the longest journey starts with a single step.

My Father is at Work

Read John 5:9-18

We mentioned yesterday about the amount of diversity of practice there was in the Jewish community 2,000 years ago. This certainly seems to have been expressed in respect of what rite to perform before eating. Some members of the community immersed themselves in water completely before sitting down to a meal. Some washed their hands. Others did neither, and felt none the worse for it. That there was also a difference of opinion about how to celebrate the Sabbath shouldn't surprise us.

When it comes to practice relating to the Sabbath, we get the strong impression that the instincts of Jesus and the religious establishment in Judea were somewhat different. In this passage today, we note that Jesus' healing of the man by the pool didn't go down well with the authorities. He had His own reasons, however. Jesus says that His Father still works, and so does He. When Jesus heals on the Sabbath He is simply following His Father's example. Like Father like Son.

So, Jesus healed on the Sabbath. That was a good thing. But the man He healed went and told the authorities that it was Jesus who had healed him. Now this was not so good, we have to admit.

When we bring glory to God and help others on the Sabbath, or on any other day, this has to be a good thing. Doing ill to others or lifting ourselves up in the presence of others, this had to be a bad thing. How different our fellowships would be if this was our watchword. We are to remember that God is on the throne. Also, we need to remember that when we lift ourselves up for others to admire, this comes at the expense of someone else. It always does. When we do that, our heart and our spiritual compass are somewhat awry. Repenting of this, however, is a good first step. When we are in the company of others, let's attempt to bless and encourage our brothers and our sisters. When we do this, on the Sabbath or on any other day, our Heavenly Father notices and is delighted.

The Authority of the Son
Read John 5:19-30

In the community to which Jesus belonged, people knew that God was their Father. There were references to this in the Greek translation of the Jewish Bible. Yet in today's reading, there is an obvious and intimate level of closeness between God, our Heavenly Father, and Jesus His Son. Jesus is uniquely God's Son, and God is uniquely His Father.

We saw yesterday that Jesus knew His Father worked on the Sabbath, and so did He. Taking His Father's thinking and practice as a template seems to have been something of a rule for Him. What He knows of the Father's activity shapes His own choices, teaching and ministry. To honour Jesus, then, is to honour the Father. The Father sent Jesus, His Son, into the world. Whoever believes in Jesus receives eternal life, not eternal condemnation. Many of the teachers who comprised the Judean religious authorities – those who self-defined as Pharisees rather than Sadducees – expected bodily resurrection after death. As we have mentioned before, there is teaching on this found in Daniel 12:2. This indicates that, for some, resurrection would be good news, whereas for others, it would not. What John teaches, here, underlines that it is our response to Jesus which really makes the difference eternally.

The Father is happy about the central role which the Son plays in salvation. Again, the Spirit doesn't draw attention to Himself, but to the Son. There are no power struggles in the Godhead, no dysfunction. The Son didn't leave His home in Heaven and come into the world because the Father was, to use the technical term, "doing His head in." The relationships between Father, Son and Spirit are normative for us. This is certainly so in the sense that when we take these divine relationships seriously, we don't obsess about our own greatness. When don't spend our days wondering whether enough people are recognizing how basically wonderful we are.

Jesus says, in verse 30, that He doesn't please Himself, but He prefers to please the One who sent Him. What a powerful message this is for us. We experience salvation so that we can bring glory to our Heavenly Father. We walk with Jesus day by day, taking His teaching with utmost seriousness. We open our heart to the Spirit of God, and the truth is that the more we do this, the more we long to be like God. Along this road, we become most fully the people we were created and saved to be. Our humanity will be at its most beautiful when we are at our most holy. Self-obsession is the definition of spiritual ugliness and lack of holiness. Our prayer needs to be that the Lord would make us more and more like Him. What a wonderful journey that is.

The Importance of Moses

Read John 5:31-47

In lots of ways, Jesus and the Pharisees occupied the same part of the Jewish landscape 2,000 years ago. That's one of the reasons the Pharisees are mentioned so often in the Gospels. They shared a high view of the Scriptures and also believed in the existence of spirits, angels and life after death. Where Jesus seems to have taken issue with them was in how to take all of this seriously in practise. It was on these kinds of issues that the rabbinic disagreement between them got really heated. When we are in a battle, it's important to know what our authority is, or we'll end up getting hopelessly lost. In the case of Jesus, the writings of the Prophets and of Moses were authoritative, which is why He turned to them so very often.

This is clearly illustrated for us in the accounts Matthew and Luke give us of the time of spiritual testing Jesus encountered in the desert (see Matthew 4:1-11 and Luke 4:1-13). Had He fallen at any of the three hurdles the devil placed before Him, His ministry would have been over before it had begun. The reason for this is that He would have effectively enthroned the devil, and our salvation would have been impossible to achieve. We note that with so much at stake, Jesus' only response to Satan was to cite the authoritative teaching of Moses. He does this as He quotes Deuteronomy 8:3; Deuteronomy 6:13 and Deuteronomy 6:16 (see Luke 4:4-12).

We find something rather significant in today's reading from John 5 as well. From early on in this Gospel, the religious authorities in Judea wanted to pin down this northern Rabbi as to what gave Him the right to teach and minister as He did. In rabbinic debate with them, He repeatedly directed their attention to the Scriptures in general, and to the Torah of Moses (Genesis to Deuteronomy) in particular (see verses 39, 45 and 46). This reliance on the teaching of Moses isn't out of character for Jesus. There are so many occasions in the four Gospels when He explains about God's intention lying behind teaching found in what Moses wrote. On other occasions He mentions a character found in those writings, Noah for example, and bases His own teaching on what this illustrates. And throughout the Gospels, He faithfully celebrates the Biblical feasts of which Moses wrote (see Leviticus 23).

The books we sometimes refer to as the Old Testament were so important to Jesus. Clearly they need to be important to us as well, if we really do intend to follow Him and His teaching. For this reason, as we engage with the Gospels and the practice of Jesus, it is good to remind ourselves of the roots of His teaching. There is the closest of links between the Old Testament and the New. When we emphasise this, we are following in the footsteps of the Rabbi, our Saviour.

FOLLOWING GOD'S TEACHING

Loving God Alone

Read Exodus 20:1-3; Deuteronomy 6:4-5

Sometimes we can be spoilt for choice. There are so many options, it's difficult to know which one to choose. Now, if we're children standing before a range of sweet containers, Pick n Mix can be wonderful. We can choose exactly the range and type of treats we like. So much sugar, so many colourings and preservatives. But when it comes to spirituality and what to worship, the Pick n Mix approach can come with real difficulties attached.

In the world in which Jesus and Paul taught, the range of gods to be worshipped must have seemed bewildering, as well. There were Greek gods, Roman gods and all the fun of the fair. And sometimes when the worshipper is in the driving seat, immorality could go on unchecked, and one's chosen deity has nothing to say about the matter. For the Children of Israel, including Jesus and Paul, however, they would have seen things very differently. There's only one God, and we are to worship Him alone.

That would have been underlined in the ten very special words God gave to His people through Moses. We begin to look at them today. The ten words, or commandments, will be found in our readings from Exodus over the next ten day. This teaching begins with the affirmation that there is only one God, and this truth is also found in the Shema, Israel's declaration of faith in God, found in Deuteronomy 6:4.

God's people had been brought up to take His revelation to Moses very seriously, and rightly so. When they entered Canaan and began to make it a place in which they could be safe at last, spiritual Pick n Mix was already practiced by others. One could worship Baal, Asherah or Molech. If that choice was made, religious prostitution and child sacrifice came with the territory. God's people were meant to stand out against that background. They were meant to be different, and all of that would flow from their devotion to the one and only God. How they lived really would matter, because the whole of life was to be lived in line with His teaching.

God had entered into a special relationship, or covenant, with His children, whom He had rescued from Egypt. It was on that foundation that they should live their lives. He didn't tie them up in loads of petty rules and regulations. What He did, instead, was to give them teaching, instruction and guidance. All of this is wrapped up in the meaning of the Hebrew word "Torah." In the light of it, life is transformed when we know there's only one God, and that He wants to shine His light on the path He stretches out before us.

That being true, we don't follow His teaching out of fear, but because we love Him. We really want to live in line with what He knows is best for us and our lives.

When God is our Saviour, we know He is one who loves us, and wants the best for us. And when we pattern our lives in line with His teaching, we're in the right place to receive all the good things He wants for us. As we mentioned earlier, we'll look at these Ten Commandments, or "ten words" in Hebrew, over the next few days. He really is our Saviour, and He always knows best, even in the practical things of life.

Let's Not Make God In Our Own Image
Read Exodus 20:4-6; 1 John 5:21

We mentioned yesterday that what God gave to Moses was teaching and instruction (Torah) rather than rules and regulations. And even when there were elements of commandment involved in this teaching, again we shouldn't rush too quickly to the assumption that this involved obedience to a myriad puzzling rules handed down by God, just because He could.

In many ways, what God is giving us through the teaching of Moses are principles to live by. We don't become machines who get programmed to obey. We end up understanding the heart of God, and what His intentions are. In the light of the guidance He gives, we naturally find our way to the good things He wants us to do. Our God doesn't merely require robotic, unquestioning obedience and compliance. He gives us wisdom for living. When we understand this teaching, or Torah, properly, we grow in our appreciation of His will and His ways. This is a revelation in which He shares the reality of His nature with His children.

Sometimes this seriously involves us avoiding even the appearance of the sinful life choices that can come with a worship of other gods. We thought yesterday about what was involved in devotion to deities like Baal, Asherah and Molech. In truth, we shudder at what was involved in practice. It was not unknown for devotees of these religions to make images of what they imagined these deities looked like; the making of images was part and parcel of the worship of such gods. This second "word" God gave to Moses made clear that His people should avoid the making of pictorial representations of Him, as the earlier Canaanites in the land did of their gods.

In many ways, then, this commandment isn't that the people of God should avoid art, creativity, and the ability to depict what they can see around them in the created order. No, it's really about being different from those who worship Baal, Asherah and Molech, and the prostitution and child murder practiced by the Canaanites. Against that background, this teaching really makes sense. In truth, it was again against the Canaanite background of unspeakable cruelty to others that Israel sought to live a holy life as described in the Torah.

Now, in a way, the second commandment asks us to think seriously about things practiced in our world which are contrary to God's teaching. That being the case, the teaching of Moses, here, asks us to stand out from the crowd. How do people try to cut God down to size these days? How do they try to domesticate Him? How do they try to justify extremely sinful practices? It's this territory which the second commandment brings to our attention.

Perhaps in a way, societies have often turned away from God, and have enthroned whatever seemed reasonable, or desirable, at the time. That option is a non-starter for the people of God. We are not to "manage" God; He is Lord over us. We are not to try to attempt to justify sin, as if that were an appropriate expression of our Creator's will. Sin always comes with consequences attached, as verse 5 of Exodus 20 suggests. But verse 6 makes clear that God is gracious, and is looking for ways of blessing us. When we attempt to put Him first, we will never go far wrong. The teaching God gave to Moses is nothing if not practical.

Not In My Name

Read Exodus 20:7; Matthew 5:33-37

These days, litigation seems to be such a feature of the dealings between people. Contracts are drawn up, and if someone's promise doesn't come to speedy fulfilment, there's always the recourse to Law. This is understandable in some ways. In many respects, though, in ancient Israel it was the taking of oaths that was designed to assure others of a person's truthfulness and trustworthiness.

The third commandment addresses this kind of situation. It counsels us not to lie or swear falsely using the name of the LORD with the intention of us getting what we want. We are not intended to fleece others using God in the process. If we do, He won't turn a blind eye to this misuse of His name.

In a sense, then, what was at stake was this. A person intended to deceive someone else. In the process, the deceiver dragged God in on his side, showing utter contempt for His holy name as he does so. Clearly, Jesus' understanding of the issues overlapped with that of Moses. In the Sermon on the Mount (Matthew 5:33-37), Jesus highlights all that's wrong with a sophisticated cuteness which attempts to use words, even holy words, to outmanoeuvre someone else. He teaches that anything beyond a straightforward Yes or No "comes from the evil one." Quite so.

God matters, and so does His name. We can't drag Him into our attempt to deceive others. If we understand the holiness of His nature and His name, we ought to be truthful people. When we are cute and clever in our use of words in the hope of stitching someone up, this shows a disregard for the other person, and for their Creator. When we ourselves are truthful, we show that we take God seriously. And that being so, we fulfil the teaching of Jesus and Moses. How great it is when believers are people others can trust.

God Blesses The Sabbath
Read Exodus 20:8-11; Matthew 24:15-20

The teaching God gives to Moses about the Sabbath is the fourth "word," or commandment. These first four speak about our relationship with Him. The six commandments which follow are about how we treat others in the light of a good relationship with God. But, what's this one about? How are we to understand a proper celebration of the Sabbath?

We're told in our reading in Exodus that this concerns the "seventh day," the name given to this day in Genesis 2:2-3. The picture which emerges from what the Ten Commandments have to say about the seventh day is about rest, holiness and a cessation of our normal patterns of daily work. Now, even if we approach the teaching, here, as being about the importance of resting on one day of the week, this is significant. When we try to keep going 24/7, we don't increase the amount of things we're able to get done. So often, we end up hitting the wall and experiencing a real meltdown in our lives. Rest is obviously important. There's more to be said about our readings today, however.

We remember in the light of Scripture, of course, that the Sabbath isn't our Saturday. It begins at sundown Friday, and ends at sundown Saturday. So often a traditional Jewish Friday evening welcoming of the Sabbath sets the tone for this day as a whole. This special day is meant to give an opportunity to delight in God, and in the quality of life and salvation He gives by His grace. The Sabbath is really about our Creator and Saviour, and how we live before Him.

In the Jewish community, it is welcomed with a special meal on the Friday evening. There is so much that is good about it. At the heart of it is a celebration of the beginning of the Sabbath, which announces that it isn't a burden, but something which is received as a delight. What a wonderful gift God has given His people in this. On such a day, we really can worship God our Saviour, and this colours the whole of our life in a good and positive way.

Thinking of this kind of snapshot of what a Sabbath day looks like for so many people, this somehow speaks to us about the privilege of being God's people. It provides this seventh day as a foretaste of a heavenly enjoyment of the presence of God. Then, on the other six days, we live and work appropriately before Him. The teaching we find in this commandment, and in the other nine, come to think of it, is about living a positive and godly life. It isn't at all like its caricature: "Thou shalt not." This teaching is positive and life affirming. It's about how we live this abundant life before our generous Heavenly Father.

Do we need to make a few changes to how we celebrate this wonderful day of rest? If we make them, the whole of our life will feel the benefit. And so will the people around us.

Honouring Our Parents

Read Exodus 20:12; Ephesians 6:1-4

This and the following five pieces of teaching Moses gives refers to our relationships with others under God. In verse 12 of Exodus 20 we read about the importance of honouring our parents so that His people may live long in the Land of Israel which He is giving them. All of this teaching from Moses shaped the understanding of Jesus and Paul; that is because they will have heard the Torah read in the synagogue each week from boyhood.

For this reason, Paul passes this on to the believers in Ephesus. He tells them to honour their parents which, he says, is the first commandment to come with a promise. This promise is that things may go well with them in their long life in the Land. He gives a practical application of this when in Ephesians 6:4 he tells the fathers in the fellowship not to be harsh in the way they discipline their children. Instead, he writes that they should raise their children in the Lord's way.

There is something really thoughtful about the teaching of Moses and Paul. The commandment to give honour to parents doesn't occur in a vacuum. It occurs in a world in which the elderly were held in high esteem, as younger members of the family cared for those who were older. In ancient Israel, and the Jewish community in the Eastern Mediterranean, the importance of the honouring of parents is enshrined in the Scriptures. This doesn't imply that it wasn't happening in practise. Instead, it helps us to understand why it did happen; God's teaching led to an appropriate love for parents.

This means that when we are particularly thoughtful towards our own parents, God notices and is pleased. Of course, this is going to mean different things in practice for each of us depending on our circumstances. Our world has changed so much. It is the global village people often talk about. Unlike very many centuries ago, we don't always live out the whole of our lives in the village in which we were born. Indeed, we might live, work and raise our own families in one part of the world, and have elderly parents in another, thousands of miles away. In this situation, honouring parents might mean Skyping on a regular basis, and helping our parents sustain a genuine relationship with their grandchildren. Marking birthdays, and arranging visits, when this is possible, could easily be what honouring our parents looks like these days.

The important thing is that we don't beat ourselves up for not being able to do the impossible. But we can care. And when we do, our parents can be blessed by our thoughtfulness.

Don't Murder

Read Exodus 20:13; Matthew 5:21-26

What's being taught today in these readings is the unacceptable nature of illegal killing. In line with the world in which ancient Israel lived, the death penalty was not unknown, in legal codes of the time. Also, it was recognized that there would be another type of the lawful taking of life during military action. These are not outlawed in the sixth commandment. The unlawful taking of life by an individual is, however. The teaching of the Torah of Moses is quite specific about what is meant, here. In Exodus 21:12-14 we are reminded that it is only the intentional, premeditated killing of a person that's in view. Accidental homicide isn't covered by this commandment, and it doesn't itself warrant the death penalty.

In lots of ways, there's something very progressive about the teaching we find in these commandments. Ancient Israel isn't permitted to live by a might-is-right kind of creed. It isn't a case of "you injure one of my family, and I'll kill one of yours." There's something very specific, measured and quite understandable about all of this. And clearly, Jesus was so committed to this teaching that He also taught about how not to infringe it in practice (Matthew 5:21-26).

He rightly locates the possibility of intentional, premeditated, killing in the mind and anger of the perpetrator. Jesus is telling us that if we root out the festering hatred one person might have for another, murder isn't going to take place, and the teaching of Moses will be followed. It's when we give in to anger, contempt and the demeaning of another person that things can grow to the point where murder might be the outward expression of what's going on inside a person.

Is there someone we strongly dislike? It might be that there is. Dealing with this inner, toxic, contempt for that person is a great place to start. Over a period of time, we might even get to the point where we can forgive that person for what they have done to us, or to one of our family or friends. Allowing things to grow and fester is never a good thing.

Paul really understood and cherished the teaching of Moses and Jesus. He also understood this commandment as well. That's why he wrote to believers in Ephesus along these lines (Ephesians 4:26-27). He told them not to sin because of anger, and to make sure they never carried anger for a person over from day to day. If they gave in to anger, they would be sure to give the devil a foothold in their thinking and in their life. That's great teaching, and super advice. And prayer is a wonderful place to start if we're intent on removing festering rage out of our lives. As we struggle with these issues, the Lord will be sure to walk with us.

Avoid Adultery

Exodus 20:14; Matthew 5:27-30

Yesterday we noticed now Jesus gave teaching about how to make sure we don't infringe one of the commandments. In the passages before us today, we find another example. Again, He locates the beginning of the breaking of the Lord's teachings in human thoughts and feelings. Jesus had taught that if people want to avoid murder they need to deal with their inner anger issues. Now He teaches that if we want to avoid the committing of adultery, we need to deal with lust, and root it out from our thinking.

Adultery begins, then, with seeing, wanting and devoting thought to the pleasure of having. What Jesus is doing, here, is giving practical advice about how to fulfil the teaching God gave to Moses. This teaching is good. It needs to be followed. And Jesus shows us how.

Lust and adultery are, in a sense, different from, and similar to, anger and murder. They are different from the path to killing, because there isn't necessarily at any stage a desire to damage others and our relationships with them when we think about sexual sin. They are similar, though, in that this path still actually does damage others, and it arrives with a cost towards us as individuals when we choose adultery. When this road has been chosen, it can end with our close relationships being shot to bits.

Wisdom entails that we avoid the circumstances in which we develop a journey to adultery. This might mean making sure we don't visit a particular person. It might also entail making sure we are busy with constructive things, and not creating an opportunity for sexual desire to lead to sin. This so often arrives with tragic consequences. Perhaps the example of King David is instructive, here (2 Samuel 11).

Certainly, as with any area of life, when we bring our lack of holiness to God, the Holy One of Israel, He is always willing and able to help us. He'll speak through the Scriptures. He'll speak through the godly advice of wise individuals who are confidential. And He'll go on filling us with His Spirit so we face human frailty with divine strength. Let's continue to cherish the Scriptures, our desire for holiness, and the wonderful relationships God has given us. And let's always ask for His help so that we can walk in His ways. Nothing comes close to the joy of this.

God Gives. We Don't Take

Read Exodus 20:15: Ephesians 4:28

The God who gave the commandments to Moses already was the Saviour of His people. He had already rescued them from slavery in Egypt (Exodus 13:17-14:31). They were by now on the safe side of the Red Sea. By this stage, He had already also provided manna, quail and water for them in the desert (Exodus 16:1-17:8). He was their provider, too.

When we grab other people's things – items God has given them – it's a crime against the people concerned. That's obvious enough. But it's also a vote of No Confidence in God and His ability to provide for us. Stealing means that we think that He isn't up to the job of providing for us; we have to do it for ourselves. When we become the takers, we are saying that it isn't sensible to trust God to be the giver.

We are not intended to take other people's things. That being so, we can see the kind of trafficking of people today as especially vile. If we can't take things, we certainly can't take people, and trap them in a modern form of slavery. Such behaviour in society cuts across social cohesion and good relationships. In a way, when I ignore this teaching, I am all that matters. Other people don't count. Indeed, things become more important to me than others, and that's no way to live.

Paul puts it so well in the teaching he gave to believers in Ephesus. He links a person choosing not to work with stealing to get by. Instead, he counsels that those who trust in the Lord should work, whenever possible, and produce something with their own hands. They are then able to help others. Other people do matter, and we are able to help them when there's a need. It shouldn't be all about me, after all.

There's no reason why, as believers, we should take an anti-materialist path. "Stuff" isn't evil; it's created and given to us by God. But, others are important, too. And as we consider their needs, we can end up living a more abundant life, with a greater sense of perspective about it all. Let's think about God as Creator and Provider. When He is in the right place in our lives, we end up living a more appropriate life. We see His finger prints on our blessings. And, it's such a blessing to give to others, as well, as Jesus taught (Acts 20:35).

Truth At All Times

Read Exodus 20:16; 3 John verses 1-4

The Bible in today's reading from Exodus tells us not to lie or give evidence against our neighbor that is false and untrustworthy. This obviously has the sense of avoiding false testimony in court. That being so, the sentiment is also intended to cover false claims of ownership. In a way, lying like this is another way of stealing something from someone using a perversion of the legal process to get the job done.

In getting down to the specifics of lying like this, Moses enjoins upon the people of God the importance of being truthful at all times. We can't be right with Him in our covenant relationship with Him, yet, at the same time, living out the opposite in our relationship with others. It's for this reason that we find a huge amount of material similar to this in the rest of Exodus, the whole of Leviticus, and the opening chapters of Numbers. When our relationship with God is as it should be, this will always be reflected in how society regulates itself.

As those who love God, we are never to be involved with bending the truth. This could take the form of falsely claiming: "I own that strip of land adjacent to our house," "I wrote that song, you didn't co-write it with me," or "That project in work is mine not ours; I'll get the credit for it, thank you very much." Alternatively, just think of the effect on others when God's people are shown to be truthful and generous in their dealings with others. When we give or share with other people, this can speak powerfully of our relationship with God; and people around us will notice. "Yes, Roberta and Jason did superb work on this project, too. It couldn't have been done without them. "

In the second of our readings today, John obviously rejoices that the person to whom he writes, Gaius, is a person of truth. He is said to walk in the truth; this is a Jewish way of saying that he lives in the truth. Our faith is based on what God has revealed to be true, in Jesus and in all of the Scriptures. Our life is in harmony with this, too. How wonderful it would be if, when people observe how we live, they might also say of us that we are people of truth.

When that's how we live, we show that we are those who produce good fruit, because our roots go down deep into the truth of what Jesus taught and modelled for us (Matthew 7:15-23). We are then those who do the kind of things our Heavenly Father wants. In the process, we have nothing to fear in this world or in the world to come. So, let's be people of truth. When we are, God sees us and is delighted.

An Insatiable Desire
Read Exodus 20:17; Philippians 4:10-13

The Ten Commandments end with counsel to avoid an insatiable desire for what isn't ours; covetousness, in a word. I know you're going to be impressed, but this material you're reading was written by someone who has never once coveted his neighbour's ox. How could you not be impressed by that? The problem for me is that that's where my virtue probably ends, when it comes to this vice. I could take or leave my neighbour's ox, but what about his books, musical instruments, upcoming cruise around the Eastern Med or my wife's Costa points? That's a bit trickier. Then covetousness comes thick and fast.

In a way, because life is never absolutely tidy with everything in its own category, desire for my neighbour's wife echoes earlier teaching about the avoidance of lust and adultery. There's also yesterday's teaching about lying in court in order to take what belongs to someone else. But for the rest in today's readings, this is more about "stuff" in the sense of possessions, and wanting more for myself. There's the neighbour's estate or business complete with domestic and other staff. This comes with the desire to be as successful as our neighbour obviously is. Beyond this, there's the thought that what belongs to my neighbour would obviously be put to better use in my hands. That's because I see myself as a quality person, unlike the uncultured social climber next door. It's all about me, not about God as the provider, and the guide of my life.

Earlier in this chapter, we mentioned how Jesus taught about us getting our thinking right so we don't commit adultery or murder. Therefore, He taught us that lust and anger need to be rooted out of our thinking and behaviour patterns. If we do this properly, we'll follow the teaching of Moses. And it's the same in these verses today. If I become obsessed with that person or thing, then I can easily end up scheming to acquire him, her or it.

When it comes to understanding the Scriptures Jesus cherished, Paul again gets it absolutely right in this area of teaching. He wrote to the Philippians, and, as we saw in today's reading, drew their attention to contentment and being at peace in God. And he knew that God was the One who helped him to do whatever it was he needed to do. God makes the difference. Truth to tell, if I'm as inwardly peaceful as the average tornado, having that ox, or whatever, isn't going to transform my life. No possession ever could. I'll be the same person after as before, and I'll be just as dissatisfied with life then as I am now. God is the answer, to inner peace, contentment, and to being thoroughly happy in life in the here and now. And that's a great place to be. With God's help, we can get there.

ROMAN JUSTICE AND GOD'S RESPONSE

Extravagant Love
Read Mark 14:1-11

In Mark's Gospel, Jesus enters Jerusalem back at the start of chapter 11. But by the time we get to today's reading in chapter 14, the storm clouds are obviously gathering for the Rabbi from Galilee. The authority of Rome, its military, and its representatives in the city, including the Chief Priest, casts a real shadow over what we read in the final three chapters of what Mark writes. With many thousands of extra people in the city for this feast, the possibility of unrest couldn't be ignored. The last thing the establishment wanted was for someone, like Jesus, to toss a match onto the explosives.

Rome indeed provides the landscape for what we will encounter in this section of the Gospel. In today's reading, though, it will be an extravagant love for Jesus which shines most brightly. The Biblical

Feast of the Passover, with its accompanying Feast of Unleavened Bread, will soon be celebrated by all observant members of Jesus' community. After all, that's why they were all in the city. In these verses, Jesus is sharing a meal with someone called Simon at his home in Bethany, nearby. An unnamed woman enters, breaks an alabaster jar of highly expensive perfume, and pours its contents over Jesus' head.

There were some present who weren't too happy about this. Let's face it, you might have noticed that whenever anything happens, some will always manage to find fault. In this case, those who were complaining couldn't see beyond the very obvious love this woman had for Jesus, her Rabbi and Saviour. The perfume, pure nard, could have been sold, and the poor could have been helped. Certainly, a sum which amounted to more than a year's wages could have been put to a different use, and that's a fair comment. Jesus rebukes those who spoke harshly to her, though. He tells them that those who have a genuine desire to help people in need will always be able to do so. This lady's affection for Him, however, will have been expressed in a one-off event. This was quite unrepeatable. She was expressing her love for Him; and He was being anointed for His burial.

All of this seems to have been just too much for one of Jesus' twelve rabbinic disciples, someone called Judas from Keriot. He went to the authorities and promised to facilitate the handover of His onetime Rabbi. From their point of view, this would take care of one potentially massive problem. If Jesus were to trigger an uprising, and let's remember He had just ridden into the city as its King, no-one knew how far the Roman military will have gone to re-establish order.

Of course, if we love God, this is going to be expressed in how we help and bless others. That ought to go without saying. There is a level of devotion to God, however, which can only be expressed by those who truly love Him. People will obviously queue up to denounce such an apparent waste of money. That place of worship might be too expensive. That level of love for Jesus might just be plain embarrassing and over the top. Without being ripped off by religious scam artists – they exist in every area of life – a heart full of love for the Lord will always be noticed by Him. So let's develop our love for Him, and express it in line with the leading of His Spirit. His "well done" is much more important than the approval of others, after all.

Passover Approaches
Read Mark 14:12-31

With the Passover approaching, Jesus sends two of His rabbinic disciples into the city of Jerusalem. Mark tells us that as they enter the city, they will see a man carrying a container of water. Was he, perhaps, one of Jesus' followers in Judea? It wasn't only Galileans who followed Him after all. This local follower showed the two disciples to a large upper room. It would be there that they would be able to celebrate their Passover meal.

Mark highlights a number of features from this celebration. One is the use of unleavened bread which was dipped into a bowl. This either contained charoset or bitter herbs, both of which are still used in Passover meals today. The Gospel of Mark also underlines the use of one of the cups of wine. Jesus draws a link between the bread and His body, and this cup and His blood. This celebration becomes a meal of covenant renewal for them, because of His approaching sacrificial death. As disciples far away from home, whose Rabbi insisted on teaching them about His impending death, they could hardly have been expected to understand what was taking place. It all must have seemed quite bewildering and overwhelming for them. Dark days certainly stood between this familiar meal, which now seemed very unfamiliar, and their restored joy at Jesus' Resurrection.

As usual, they concluded their celebration with the singing of Psalms 113-118. They then set out for the Mount of Olives which lay to the east of the city across the Kidron Valley. Clearly, none of the disciples could envisage denying Jesus; how could they? What we see in all of this with equal clarity is the grace of God which restores us. This is the case even when our fine words aren't matched by fine and faithful deeds.

In all sorts of ways we let God down with alarming regularity. We note this not in order to increase our levels of guilt, but to assure ourselves about His level of love for us. If God were looking for opportunities to catch us out and reject us, it really wouldn't take Him very long. That's a fact. Thankfully that isn't His purpose. In these verses, brittle disciples are seen approaching the moment their faith will break. However, we consider these events in the light of the God who delights in restoring us. At the end of the day, our relationship with the Lord isn't sustained by our ability to talk a good game. We can thank God for that. It's sustained by His desire to be faithful to us. How wonderful it is to be reassured by this truth.

Taken to the Limit

Read Mark 14:32-52

In today's verses we are told about Jesus taking His core rabbinic disciples, Peter, James and John, into the Garden of Gethsemane at the foot of the Mount of Olives. In this very moving account, Mark describes Him being taken to the limit as He prayed. He knows what is coming, but He trusts His Abba, His Heavenly Father, to sustain Him and bring Him through. Jesus continues to pray, but the three succumb to sleep, their spirit being willing to watch and pray with Him, but the flesh being weak.

One of the twelve disciples appeared with armed personnel sent by the Judean authorities. In this way, the Rabbi from Galilee is handed over to those who govern the life of the city of Jerusalem under the authority of Caesar. Jesus wonders why they are armed. He had been with them daily in the Temple courts as He taught the people. He mentions the fact that they could have arrested Him then, any time they wanted to. Jesus sees how things are working out, however, as the fulfilment of Scripture. He knows that He will be raised from the dead and vindicated by His Father, but He will need to trust every step of the way, as He experiences the grim reality of a Roman execution.

The things we face in life are obviously not comparable to the dreadful things Jesus faced. That's true when we bear in mind the awful physical death He was to die, and the extent to which the sin of the world was laid upon Him. He experienced its terrible reality, but He remained sinless Himself. Though our sufferings will not be of the same order, this isn't noted in order to minimise the dark difficulties through which some of us go from time to time. The truth is that in such situations, we will need to trust our Heavenly Father every step of the way, as well. And Jesus shows how we can trust God, for the Scriptures were in His mind and heart right the way through.

In these chapters, there are so many allusions to the earlier Scriptures, as we would expect. We know that what happened to Jesus wasn't the result of the coming together of haphazard events. The steps Jesus took were not unforeseen by our Heavenly Father. Far from it. Peter would put it perfectly a number of years later (1 Peter 1:19-20) when he describes His Saviour as the Lamb who was chosen before the creation of the world.

This truth reminds us that our salvation was meticulously planned, and a long time coming. That's how much God loved us and provided a remedy for your sins and mine. As this horrible Roman execution played itself out, individuals played their part. That's true. But in every conceivable way, God really was the principal Actor, the active Player. We can certainly thank Him for that. Who put Jesus on the Cross? Ultimately, it was neither Judeans nor Romans. It was God.

Jesus Appears Before the Authorities
Read Mark 14:53-72

In the final section of chapter 14, Peter seems increasingly desperate to put distance between himself and Jesus. At the same time we see the Rabbi from Galilee appearing before the authorities in Judea. Mark reminds us that all of this action takes place in the context of the delegated authority the Judean establishment had from Rome. He will go on to focus more specifically on the power of Rome in the next chapter, but even here we need to remember that the Chief Priest was a Roman appointee. He was part politician, part religious official in Judea. Even seen as a focus of unity for the great and the good in the Judean establishment, he was still Rome's man.

What the Chief Priest administers for Caesar is the good order of the religious life in an around Judea. Bearing in mind that there are always security issues for a place like Jerusalem, when anything in the religious sphere spins out of control, this is an affront to Rome. The problem must be shut down, and shut down quickly. Now in many ways, that reality helps us to understand the behaviour of the Chief Priest as the troublesome Rabbi from Galilee is brought to stand before him.

If the action in today's reading had taken place centuries earlier, when Israel was self-governing, truth to tell, there wouldn't been too much of a problem with Jesus' self-understanding. In today's reading, He illustrates the silence of the suffering servant of God as found in Isaiah 53:7. Then, when pushed to clarify whether He sees Himself as the Messiah, He confirms this and describes the heavenly aspect of what all of this means. He will sit at the right hand of God, and will appear at the end of time in the Father's glory.

A claim to Messiahship in itself isn't a problem, and doesn't lead automatically to the giving of the death penalty. There were many before and since who have made such claims without paying for them. When Rome is the only show in town, however, and someone claims kingly authority as the anointed Messiah, that can't be allowed to stand. So Jesus receives the only sentence which was possible.

Rome expects good order in the religious sphere, and the One who threatens it must be handed over to Rome so He can be dealt with. Bearing in mind the very obvious power of Rome in Jerusalem 2,000 years ago, the Chief Priest couldn't possibly have defended Jesus, or identified with Him. Neither could Peter who also puts distance between himself and his Rabbi. At the end of the day, Peter was acting from motives that were similar to that of the Chief Priest. This rabbinic disciple denied Jesus because he was worried about his own neck, and what the soldiers would do to him, too.

What this puts on the table for us are the times when we didn't identify with Jesus. Let's face it, all sorts of people cast their shadow over our family life, our friendship circles and employment experience. A simple question like: "What did you do over the weekend?" can come with difficulties attached. We've all been there. We've all done it. We might be happy to describe 80% of what we got up to – the shopping, the gym and the meal at the latest, greatest venue. But are we as relaxed at acknowledging that our faith in God meant that we also went with others to worship, so that we could be taught more about the Lord? This might be a bit too much for us, with those particular individuals listening. I've fallen at this hurdle as well on countless occasions.

Others obviously have authority to a certain extent in the here and now in this world. Sometimes, that's as it should be, for the most part. And many who have authority have been appointed by God, whether they know it or not. However, when we have denied the Lord, because this would have been beyond embarrassing, there is always a way back for us. He will always restore us, when we come to Him in repentance. The Gospels and the Book of Acts indicate the extent to which Peter was restored. And this can be such an encouragement to us. Putting distance between ourselves and Jesus doesn't have to be the end. Far from it. God was always the One who comes looking for us, as He did back in the Garden for Adam (Genesis 3:9). His question "Where are you?" is intended to invite our return and repentance. In the light of this, we have no need to allow the devil to fuel our ongoing estrangement from God.

Jesus Appears Before Pilate
Read Mark 15:1-15

Jesus now stands before the Roman Governor, Pontius Pilate. He had been handed over to him by the Chief Priest's council, which was Judea's religious authority. Pilate gets straight to the matter in hand as he asks Jesus "Are you the King of the Judeans?" That's the central issue for an official who can only see Caesar in authority. There's no room for anyone else to muscle in. Though there are all sorts of things Pilate asks, he is only really concerned about this issue of rival kingship. Is He a Judean King or not?

The Chief Priest's council isn't interested in having Jesus released. They can't be. Anyone else's release is fine, but Jesus can't be allowed to damage the amount of relative freedom the Judeans have on religious issues. Jesus has to be dealt with so that things don't spin out of control, ending with the destruction of the Temple. This fear wasn't unfounded, because that's exactly what happened just a few decades later. That's exactly what the Romans would do in a heartbeat, and everyone knew it. The Rabbi made Himself King of the Judeans, so now He has to pay the price exacted by Caesar. A number of Judeans gathered to make sure that this Galilean didn't spoil things for them. He must be flogged, then handed over to the execution squad. And so He was. Mark confirms this in a fairly matter of fact way in verse 24. He tells us about the actions of these Roman soldiers, then simply records: "And they crucified Him."

Now of course, it's right that we should have tried to understand all of this against its proper historical background. We've needed to think about what the issues were for the leadership in Judea, religious, political and military. When all is said and done, however, we principally reflect upon the awful price the Lamb of God paid for your sins and mine. We are familiar with all of this to a certain extent. And familiarity often takes away our wonder and gratitude. There's always the danger that we think of this wonderful Atonement as some kind of religious equation. Jesus' death for our sins does indeed mean that our sins have been dealt with. This is not to say, however, that we can ever be relaxed and blasé about it all. And we certainly can't, on that foundation, be casual about ongoing sin, as if it doesn't matter, because it's already been dealt with. Yes, it has been, but sin is still toxic, and it damages us and those around us. Sin isn't consequence free. Looking at Jesus on the Cross shows us that with all possible clarity.

Indeed, sin has already been dealt with. The truth is, however, that we were also saved for something, not only from something. As citizens of Heaven here on earth, we are saved for a life of holiness. That being so, a casual attitude towards ongoing sin is, at best, counterproductive, and, at worst, something which saddens our Heavenly Father. We wouldn't intentionally sadden members of our families or our closest friends whom we love. We'd do whatever we could not to cause such distress. It is important, too, that we don't presume to sadden God, who loves us more than anyone ever could. Let's make His pleasure our chief delight, in all things.

A Roman Death

Read Mark 15:16-32

Roman soldiers now gather at the Governor's residence. Though Mark informs us about the crucifixion of Jesus in just a few words in verse 24, as we noted yesterday, he describes what the Messiah now faces in some detail. Those who belonged to Rome's military presence in Judea mock Jesus. They don't do this because they don't particularly like His teaching. After all, they are not qualified to assess His application of the Torah teaching of Moses, which formed the substance of what He taught. They mock Him for the only thing that matters to them, to Caesar, to Pilate, and to Caesar's appointed Chief Priest, namely, His claim to kingship. If He thinks He is the Messiah, then He must think He's a Judean King, the King of Israel (verses 18 and 32). And that's an affront to Rome.

So Mark tells us about the mock reverence the soldiers pay to this self-appointed King. It's all there: the royal robe, the crown, and the cries of homage. There's only one thing for someone to face when they think they can take on the Emperor but can't apparently even save themselves from being put to death by members of his military. As we're told in verse 20, they led Him out to crucify Him. The soldiers saw the action in the light of the here and now. They understood it all simply in terms of the authority of Caesar, someone who would be in power in Rome today, but would be followed by someone else in due course.

Mark knows the truth. Right back in the first verse of his Gospel he identifies Jesus properly. He is the Messiah (in Greek: the Christ), the Son of God. Jesus is the Holy One of God (chapter 1 verse 24) who has the authority to cast out demons. He truly is the Judean King, the King of Israel as we read in today's passage. Those who gave Him mock reverence will, as Paul wrote, one day stand before Him, and there will be no doubting His authority then (Philippians 2:9-11). And the same is the case for those who misunderstood what He taught about His death and resurrection, and took it to be a promise to destroy the Temple complex and rebuild it all in just three days. Clearly, Jesus could have saved Himself from such a shameful death. Had He done so, this would have been at our expense, as He knew. He wasn't there because He had taken on Caesar and it had all gone wrong for Him. He was there solely for us. The eternal truth remains that there is no other name than the name of Jesus which can save us (Acts 4:12).

The picture, in what Mark details today, is that when He died for us, people were heaping insults at Him. As those who are privileged to call Him our Saviour and Lord, we will give Him something else, namely, all the praise. We can't begin to imagine the lengths to which He was prepared to go in His love for us. We acknowledge Him as our King, and in heaven it will be our greatest delight to bow before Him and worship. As we worship Him in our heart day by day, we affirm His Kingship, and we ask for His help so that we can live under His authority in the meantime.

Truly Dead, Soon to be Raised

Read Mark 15:33-47

Jesus on the Cross continues to affirm His faith in His Heavenly Father. With the words: "My God, My God, why have You forsaken Me?" He loudly begins to pray Psalm 22 as we are told in verse 34.

Now, at first sight, this seems to imply anything but faith on Jesus' part. If we read it casually, it's almost as if these words imply that the Father can't be relied upon when His Son needs Him most. But David H. Stern's comment on this is really important (The Jewish New Testament Commentary, note on Matthew 27:46). He reminds us that "in Judaism, when a Bible verse is cited its entire context is implied." What Jesus is doing here, then, is praying the whole of what this Psalm contains, not just the first verse. Knowing that Psalm 22 ends in vindication by God for the one who is praying, on the lips of Jesus these are words of trust and faith. Yes He will certainly soon die. With equal certainly, however, He knows this will not be the end, Psalm 22 tells Him so.

What He is securing for us, with His death, is that forgiven sinners will be able to approach our Heavenly Father with equal certainty at all times. Mark underlines this for us when he writes in verse 38 that with the death of Jesus the "curtain of the Temple was torn in two, from top to bottom." The writer of the Letter to the Hebrews spells it out for us (Hebrews 10:19-22). He teaches that because of Jesus' death and resurrection, we are able to approach the Father with confidence and complete assurance because of our faith in Him. This was won for us because Jesus secured our right to enter Heaven – the Most Holy Place – through the curtain of His body.

This was God's doing. He opened this access for us "from top to bottom," as Mark puts it (15:38). Now we are able to have appropriate confidence because of what the death of Jesus has achieved for us. Both Mark here, and the writer of the Letter to the Hebrews, are focussing on the Heavenly Temple and are using picture language about the Tabernacle in the wilderness (Exodus 26:33). This Gospel doesn't note this tearing of the curtain to indicate God's hatred for the Temple standing in Jerusalem. It is noted to underline the certainty of our right to enter the Heavenly Temple. We can praise Him for that.

We also read in today's verses that Jesus' body was wrapped in a linen cloth, in line with Jewish practice. A senior Judean religious leader called Joseph, from Ramathaim, buried Jesus himself to indicate his faith in Him. The expectation, in burying Jesus respectfully, was that He would be raised from the dead with everyone else at the end of time. All graves would then be open. Our Heavenly Father had other ideas.

He is Risen
Read Mark 16:1-8

It is the Passover, and the Sabbath has now ended. Genesis refers to the day in question, our Sunday, as the first day of the week, so named in chapter 1 verse 5. Mark himself names it in line with the practice of the Book of Genesis. Mary from Madgdala, Mary the mother of James, and Salome come to the tomb with spices so that they can anoint the body of Jesus, because of their belief in a future resurrection for everyone, in line with Scripture. Not surprisingly they're wondering who will roll the stone away from the mouth of the tomb for them.

When they get there, however, they not only find the stone rolled away, they also see a young man dressed in a white robe. They are alarmed, and let's face it we can understand why. Was he an angel? If that's what Mark has in mind, this echoes a belief in angels by the vast majority of the Children of Israel at the time. Certainly this isn't what you expect to find when you go to anoint the body of your recently deceased Rabbi.

What they don't find in all their alarm is the body of Jesus. The young man explains why. He tells them that Jesus, who had been crucified, has been raised from the dead. The resurrection of everyone at the end of time has already begun with Him. That's why Paul referred to His resurrection as the "first fruits of those who slept" (1 Corinthians 15:20). The young man goes on to show the women the empty place where Jesus had been laid. They are to tell His disciples including Peter that He is going ahead of them back to Galilee. They will see Him there. Today's passage ends with Mark's comment that the women were afraid and ran quickly from the tomb.

How convincing it is that Mark doesn't airbrush this understandable fear and bewilderment out from this first account of faith in the risen Jesus. The women responded the way you and I would almost certainly have ourselves. We don't in any way sit in judgement on the way they responded to all of this. We read Mark's words in the light of 2,000 years' worth of belief in the Resurrection of Jesus. The women, here, didn't have that luxury. They were bereaved, bewildered and far from home. It must have seemed, to them, that things were unravelling quickly.

Their life changing experience of the risen Jesus started just where it did. That can be an encouragement to us, it really can. When something amazing and significant is happening, we don't always understand with any clarity. Certainly not at first. We can be confused and not a little afraid, and the great thing is that we don't need to try to hide this from the Lord and pretend we've got it all buttoned down.

Is something unsettling happening in our lives at present? We don't have to deny it if it is. We can give it to God – the Father who raised Jesus from the dead in the power of the Spirit. We can trust Him to accompany us on the journey to greater understanding. There we will find that understandable bewilderment can give way to praise and thanksgiving. In our very own Galilee, where we'll see Jesus, it really can be OK, and very much better than OK. Now and always, He knows what He's doing. That's why we can trust Him, whatever's going on at the moment, and however we feel.

Greater Perspective
Read Mark 16:9-20

Chances are that the Bible you are using for your daily readings at the moment contains a particular note about the verses we are looking at today. Virtually every major translation of Scripture contains such a note. This tells us that most, earlier, manuscripts of Mark's Gospel end with yesterday's reading at chapter 16 verse 8. The reading for today tends not to be included; this passage features in later documents. As a result, some believe these verses are part of the Gospel of Mark, some think otherwise. As with most things, to use the vernacular, you pays your money and you takes your choice. For my money, these verses are printed in our Bibles; they contain very ancient material, and the content is superb. For these reasons, they repay our prayerful study.

Verse 8 ends up with the first people to be informed by God about the Resurrection of Jesus, a group of women, fleeing from the tomb in understandable fear and trembling. Had we been there, we would have responded in the same way. Verses 9-20 give greater perspective about all of this, and are probably written a little later. This account tells us that when Mary from Magdala told the rest of the rabbinic disciples of Jesus, they didn't believe it either. Resurrection was expected at the end of time after all. Why would Jesus be resurrected so soon after His death? It didn't make sense.

Echoing Luke 24, we are then told about the two disciples who were on the road to Emmaus just outside Jerusalem. These also are told about the Resurrection, this time by Jesus Himself. They return to the city and tell the eleven disciples, and they still don't believe it. He then appeared to them as they were eating, and rebuked them for their stubborn refusal to believe. He commissions them to proclaim the Good News about Himself to everyone. This is in line with prophetic writings in the Scriptures that one day, people who are not Jewish at all will come flooding to the Holy One of Israel and associate themselves with the Children of Israel. For example, Isaiah had invited the nations to come to the one and only God (Isaiah 45:22): "All you ends of the earth, turn to Me and be saved; I am God, there is no other."

The message will go out to everyone, and this is in harmony with the earlier Scriptures. Those who believe in Jesus will be immersed in water and will be saved. Those who refuse the Lord's offer will be condemned. In a sense, this echoes the message of Psalm 1, that there are two ways, as God sees it. The Lord's righteous people will flourish; those who reject Him will be judged and will perish. Today's reading ends by teaching about the Ascension of Jesus to the right hand of God. He will validate the proclamation of the disciples with signs that confirm His Word. Again, this picture of the lifting up of the Messiah to the Lord's right hand is an allusion to another Psalm (110:1).

After the turbulence and confusion of early days, immediately after the Resurrection of Jesus, came greater perspective. The Ascension of the Messiah is understood in the light of Scripture, and today's reading gives a kind of big picture panoramic conclusion to what Mark has written. This section again invites us to feast on the Scriptures and to understand what God is doing in the light of them. When we lack clarity, we can pray, and our Heavenly Father can explain what we have gone through with the benefit of a kind of eternal hindsight. This helps us see the pattern and the purpose in what He has done and what He has allowed. We can always trust in Him. Early on we might be unable to see the wood for the trees. As we pray, however, greater perspective can arrive. This can come with time and God's grace.

RUTH, THE IDEAL CONVERT

No Bread In The House Of Bread
Read Ruth 1:1-7

Under God, a Moabite woman called Ruth is the central character in this book which bears her name. The significant thing is that in today's reading, Ruth is one of a number of people. And on paper, at least, we wouldn't assume that she would end up quite so central; after all, she doesn't belong to the Children of Israel. God has other ideas, however, and her journey into the things of God is an encouragement to us all. The action in this wonderful book takes place in the dim and distant past, before Israel was ruled by kings.

As the story begins, there's a famine in and around Bethlehem. Who'd have thought it? The Hebrew original of the name, Beit-Lechem, means "the House of Bread." There's nothing for it but to travel to Moab, a journey of some 60 miles. I initially thought I'd Google the distance Naomi, her husband and sons had to travel. It's always good to give background information to a passage so that we can understand it better. Surprise doesn't cover it when a website told me their journey was over 7,000 miles. I was reassured when I realised they'd calculated the distance between Bethlehem and Moab in Utah. Quite. So, it was 60 miles, not 7,000 miles, but even that's not to be sniffed at; it's still quite a trek for a family.

Naomi's family settled in Moab, and were able to find food. Her two sons married local women, but soon, the two sons and their father died. As the reading ends today, the three women begin to make preparations for the return journey to the House of Bread, Bethlehem, because the famine had come to an end. The Lord had come to the aid of His people (verse 6), which meant they could go back to Judah.

Certainly in Bible times, people took it as read that God was involved in every area of life. They could pray about famine, because famine wasn't simply the end result of the coming together of certain factors. God was somehow involved. And when the famine ended, the Children of Israel believed that God had shown mercy to them; prayer was answered.

Now of course, we know that sometimes there are natural explanations for many of the things that happen in our world. Faith doesn't mean that we have to reject what is known as a result of scientific enquiry. We are the poorer, however, if we are encouraged to assume that God isn't an active player in His world, simply because science rightly tells us certain things. We need to live wisely and look after our world, of course. But we also need to continue to pray about the natural world, the international scene, what's happening in our nation, and in your life and mine. As we pray, we can then notice that He answers prayer. He really does, because He cares, and He works with His people as Adam and Eve were supposed to work with Him right back at the beginning of Genesis.

It's good to pray about spiritual and religious things, of course. But it's also important to pray about everything else as well. God doesn't get baffled by complicated things. And there's something encouraging to our faith when we recognize that prayer gets answered. As we look at our lives, we'll be able to see the hand of God at work. There's a great deal, I'm sure, which will speak to us of His activity and blessing.

Feeling Bitter In Unpleasant Times
Read Ruth 1:8-22

Today's reading is a real gem. Naomi now turns her attention to her home town, the famine there having ended. The two daughters-in-law of Naomi are invited by her to remain in their own land, with their families and their gods. Naomi's thinking is quite clear. If they returned to Bethlehem with her, the likelihood of future husbands for them in her family would be negligible. One of the two, Orpah, does the sensible thing and stays, but Ruth comes to a different conclusion. She decides to accompany her mother-in-law, to join her people, and to convert to worship of the God of Israel. Her words of conversion in verse 16 are so beautiful. She knows the cost, and the permanence of the commitment she decides to make.

She is no longer Ruth the Moabite, worshipper of one of Moab's gods. She is Ruth, member of the Children of Israel, in covenant with the Holy One of Israel. That's quite a change. Indeed, because of the far-reaching nature of her conversion, she ends up right in the centre of God's eternal purposes. She would become an ancestor of the great King David, as the end of this short book tells us. That means something else as well, of course. Ruth is also an ancestor of Jesus the Messiah, our Saviour (Matthew 1:5).

If much faith is demanded of her, the same could be said of her mother-in-law Naomi. It must have been so difficult for her to return to her home village. She had left with the future stretching out before her and her family; how different for her now. Her husband and sons are dead. One of her two daughters-in-law preferred to stay in Moab; only these two women walked into Bethlehem many years after her departure. Naomi puts it succinctly in today's verses. Earlier, her Hebrew name, Naomi, which meant Pleasant, seemed appropriate. But now, she prefers the name Mara, Hebrew for Bitter.

Let's face it, there are even times in the life of a believer when we can carry the weight of loss, disappointment and bitterness. Bringing this to God, being honest about it in prayer, is a good way to deal with the reality of how we can sometimes feel. Pretending otherwise, denial, to put it another way, isn't an expression of faith. What denial does is increase the possibility that we get stuck in bitterness and anger at God. Being honest before Him is always wise.

If that's where we are in life because of something quite shattering that has happened to us, admitting it, and praying accordingly, are crucial. Then we'll be able to face the future with healing, and the reality of God's practical help. The picture for these two women at the end of the Book of Ruth is so positive. My hunch, however, is they might have ended up in an altogether darker place had they not come to the Lord with total honesty. He was able to help them, as He is able to help us.

So let's pray honestly. Then we might easily be surprised at how God works things out for us in the end. He never plays tricks on us. We can depend on His goodwill and faithfulness at all times whatever our circumstances look like in the short term. This means that we can always trust in Him.

God Gets To Work
Read Ruth 2:1-13

God now gets to work in Ruth's life in rather a specific kind of way. With the beginning of chapter 2 of this book, we are introduced to a relative of her former father-in-law. His name is Boaz, and he is obviously well to do. He is the owner of an estate in which she now goes to work. Her ability to pick up leftover grain on the estate stands between her and Naomi, and real hunger and poverty.

The Lord is invoked in a greeting he gives to his harvesters, and in their reply. Boaz notices Ruth and finds out who she is. In their first conversation, he shows kindness to her, and looks out for her safety. Realising who she is, he is now aware that Ruth is the young woman who has shown particular kindness, herself, to Naomi, his relative. He expects the Lord, to whom she has come for protection and help, to prosper her, to richly reward her, and to bless her. Boaz is aware that God would want to do no less than all of that for His covenant people.

These verses are richly packed with so much super teaching. They introduce us to what's involved when we are in covenant with the Lord, the God of Israel. Boaz is rightly aware that the blessing God gives is very this-worldly, and we are to be as well. The journey on which these two women have embarked is a journey to abundance, to knowledge of a generous God, and to a society in which God's people look out for others and help them. Ruth knows she has found favour with Boaz, because God has made it so.

In Biblical books like this one, not to mention Esther, Ezra, Nehemiah and many more, there's a wonderful overlap between God's activity and ours. We have the sense that His people live in the light of the reality of His presence and activity. They do what they prayerfully need to do. But in whatever they do, they seek His will, blessing and favour. This even comes through in Esther, where God isn't specifically mentioned. But He's certainly mentioned in Ruth, and she lives secure in the knowledge that He is so different from the gods of the other nations roundabout.

We also need to try to get the balance right in our lives. He is the One who guides, blesses and gives favour. Yet we are the ones who, having prayed, are expected to be active as we go about our daily lives. When there are issues in our lives, as there clearly were for Ruth and Naomi, we are expected to do what we should. Over and above this, however, God is sought by us because He really makes all the difference in our lives. And because of God, we can live without fear, knowing that He is truly going before us, and looking out for us. We could expect nothing less of our faithful, covenant God.

The Kinsman-Redeemer
Read Ruth 2:14-23

So, God begins to show His abundant care for Ruth and Naomi through Boaz, the well-to-do owner of the estate. Naomi says to her daughter-in-law about Boaz: "May the Lord bless him." In verse 20 she identifies him as one of the family's kinsmen-redeemers, someone the Lord might soon use to bring blessing and practical help.

The teaching of Moses tells us that the kinsman-redeemer plays a particular role in caring for those who had fallen on hard times (see Deuteronomy 25:5-6 and Leviticus 25:25). Not only was it customary for those in need in ancient Israel to receive food and clothing when this was required, but the kinsman-redeemer was tasked with providing more long term, problem-solving, care.

In many ways, the role of the kinsman-redeemer introduces the whole Biblical theme of redemption; our gracious God is merciful and this shines through in this little book. And in the light of God's mercy and grace Naomi made a wonderful journey from bitterness to an experience of abundance and real joy.

I often think that so many of the short books in Scripture pack a real punch. This one certainly does, as we are seeing. The salvation God gives affects how we are in this world, as well as in the world to come. That being so, there are often times when other people become part of the way in which God answers our prayers. Boaz was part of the answer to the prayers of Naomi and Ruth, in a particular kind of way.

Of course, we're not to jump to the conclusion that He wants us all to run off and marry someone by the end of the week in order to answer their prayers. Perhaps not. That's hardly a considered response to this wonderful little book. But He might indeed want us to express His kindness and mercy towards someone in our circle of influence nonetheless. We might be the right people to offer practical, tangible help, in line with the teaching of Scripture and sanctified common sense, that is. When we pray for those in need, God might want us, on occasions, to move beyond the thought "someone should do something" and to embrace the realisation that that "someone" might be me. And when we correctly hear God in this kind of situation, others can end up thanking God for His kindness and mercy.

Before we conclude our consideration of this passage, let's remember the One who, in His sacrificial death for our sins, showed Himself to be our Kinsman-Redeemer. Jesus not only came to teach in the most awesome way, He also came to unlock the door to Heaven for us, as our sins are forgiven by His saving blood. Help in this world is great and important, it really is. But saving, eternal, help is even more wonderful. Let's thank our Father that He loved us so much that He proved it in His only Son.

Another Step

Read Ruth 3:1-13

Naomi has an understanding about how things are going to work themselves out in respect to their relative Boaz. She explains it all to Ruth, her daughter-in-law. And Ruth agrees to follow Naomi's advice. If all goes as it should, Boaz might easily end up acting as their kinsman-redeemer.

In what we read, here, something very human and, potentially, intimate is being described. That can hardly be denied. Yet Ruth's actions also underline the reality of her conversion to the God of Israel, on whom she relies throughout.

Boaz works, then eats, and lies down to sleep. During the night, he discovers Ruth lying at his feet, obviously not a routine occurrence. She identifies herself to him; he is the kinsman-redeemer for her. In asking that he spreads the corner of his garment over her, this implies a proposal of marriage. Boaz is willing to follow this course of action, but tells her that there is a closer relative who has the right to act a redeemer before him (verses 12-13). If this relative refuses, then Boaz will act as kinsman-redeemer, and they will marry. To find out what happens with that relative, we will need to wait for what's narrated in chapter 4 of this book.

There's obviously something practical involved in today's verses. All of this is convincingly human, and completely in harmony with the practice of the Children of Israel. Ruth and Naomi will be cared for, and this will happen because Ruth is the ideal convert to the faith of her new people, Israel. It is noticeable that these two women are the active players in these events. Whoever we are, we can fully play our part in the life of the people of God. In the process, we can also find that He is fully our God. He doesn't keep us at arms' length. We are His, and He is ours. And there's something very close, very intimate about our relationship with Him. Without doubt, that's such a wonderful thing.

The Conversation Of Ruth And Naomi
Read Ruth 3:14-18

Ruth remained with Boaz until early morning, then went home before anyone could be any the wiser. She briefed Naomi about developments, including his gift to her of six measures of barley. This was a gift from the intended bridegroom to the woman who was, in effect, the parent of the one he wished to marry.

Naomi is aware that things will be sorted out one way or another later that day; she knows that Boaz won't rest until their future circumstances are decided. In a real sense, as we have mentioned before, God is the One who will really make the decisions. In 3:9, Ruth had asked Boaz to spread his robe over her. Yet ultimately, it would be the Lord who would really provide protection and real practical help. Ruth, Naomi and Boaz had been active in their own way; they all needed to play their part. But the Lord was working out His purposes for them and for their lives.

As we have recognized, Naomi knew that things would be settled soon. They could have a real assurance that the right thing would be done, because of the confidence they had in God. From a human point of view, things can often seem to be up in the air for us. We are not exactly sure what's going to happen in every last detail. But we can rest secure in the fact that it will all end well, when the matter has been settled with God in prayer. We can leave things with Him. When we trust Him, we know that He will work it all out for the good of His plans and purpose. Paul understood that, as we see in Romans 8:28. He will be actively working everything out in line with His purposes. When His will is our chief delight, we can rest secure in all that God is doing as well.

It's easy to trust God when we understand everything, and can see what He's doing with some clarity. The important thing is to trust Him when things still seem a little unclear. Now, in a way, Abraham will have needed to do that when he set out on his own journey of faith, of which we read in the early verses of Genesis 12. For people of faith like us, trusting Him is possible when we know that He is good, He longs to bless us, and His sovereign plan will ultimately become a reality in our lives. As Naomi says in verse 18, Boaz won't rest until it's all settled. And neither will God. We can always depend upon that.

Signed, Sealed And Delivered
Read Ruth 4:1-12

The wellbeing of widows was a matter of particular importance in ancient Israel. We can understand that at a time when the family would have had a responsibility for all of its members. If a husband died, his brother or another close relative would marry the bereaved wife, thus ensuring that she didn't fall upon hard times. In addition to this, future children would help to keep the name of the deceased alive.

This forms the background to the situation which Naomi, Elimelech's widow, and Ruth, her daughter-in-law, faced. We found yesterday that Boaz was a relative of Naomi and Ruth, but not the closest. For this reason, another person enters the action today. Would he marry Ruth and also take on the land once owned by Elimelech? We are told that this was not possible, because in doing this, difficulties would be raised for his own estate.

Boaz, the kinsman-redeemer, ends up protecting Naomi's family, and providing for its future. And all of this would happen even though, at one stage, the future looked decidedly bleak for them. The dark days of famine and bereavement end up giving way to abundance and provision well into the future.

But there's more. We remember that Ruth was once a Moabite, and that she converted to worship the God of Israel. Verse 11 shows how completely she is considered part of the people of God. Ruth is considered a person of no less standing than the matriarchs of old, Rachel and Leah. Certainly, Ruth's situation is totally transformed. This wasn't done as part of a short cut or quick fix, however. The situation moved forward in line with the teaching God gave to His people. Everything was signed, sealed and delivered in an appropriately legal fashion as well.

In the same way, God isn't depending on short cuts and quick fixes for us either. He wants only the best for us, and there is intended to be a link between this and our good practice and willingness to do things properly. God doesn't want us to be spiritual chancers who deceive others yet hope, somehow, to get lucky. There is to be a link between who we are becoming in God, and the kind of things we are able to receive from Him. And tomorrow we will notice the fullness of the plans God has for Ruth.

Beyond Her Wildest Dreams
Read Ruth 4:13-22

This fabulous little book comes to a close with Ruth experiencing the abundant life God had always wanted for her. She ends up co-owning the estate with Boaz, her husband. What we also find in today's verses is that she is able to be a blessing to Naomi, who, let's face it, had experienced more than her own share of difficulty and hardship.

Ruth also ends up becoming an ancestor of King David, one of the greatest kings Israel ever had. Matthew also spells out what that means for you and me (Matthew 1:5); she was also an ancestor of Jesus, our Messiah and Saviour. What a privilege this was for someone who began life outside of the community of the Children of Israel.

And what a journey she had been on. Ruth had experienced a welcome into the life of a family which worshipped the Holy One of Israel. This happened when she married for the first time. With Naomi, she arrived in Bethlehem of Judah, and was welcomed by the locals. She was welcomed by Boaz, and ended up playing the full role in things that God wanted for her. At no point did she experience rejection by the people of God. We can also say that she didn't opt to live a life of passivity, pitying herself and wondering what God might do for her out of the blue.

In later years, this book was very much part of the Scriptures that were cherished by Jesus and Paul. It spoke of a community in which both men and women were highly valued, and non-Jews were welcome at the Temple in Jerusalem. They were also welcome throughout the life of the people of God. Ruth was the ideal convert, and so many people have come to God, following her example.

Perhaps this book asks us to turn our gaze away from ourselves and our immediate needs, to those around us who might value the welcome we can give them. So often in life, as we help others we find a kind of fulfilment that can't be ours if we take the path of the self-obsessed. Ruth shows us a better way; and without doubt, the blessing will be ours as we take it.

JESUS, GLORY AND BELIEF – THE LAST FOUR SIGNS IN JOHN'S GOSPEL

The Feeding of the 5,000

Read John 6:1-15

A little while ago we looked together at the first three signs Jesus performed in John's Gospel (2:1-5:47). Towards the end of this section He spoke about the link between a natural understanding of the teaching of Moses and acceptance of His own ministry (5:45-47). We are now going to look at the final four of Jesus' signs (6:1-12:50). As we take this up at the beginning of chapter 6, John again underlines the overlap between the Scriptures which were accepted by the Jewish community and Jesus' ongoing ministry.

The Rabbi from Galilee has crossed the Sea of Galilee, ascended a mountainside, and sits down in true rabbinic fashion to teach the disciples. John's mention of Jesus on the mountain is significant. Often there is a significant meeting with God in Scripture when mountains are mentioned. Today's reading in John chapter 6 is no different. John notes that a large crowd approached Jesus, and He asked one of His disciples, Philip, how they could feed such a multitude. Philip saw the scale of the problem and how much it would cost to give each of them a little to eat. Jesus already knew what He would do.

Andrew drew the Rabbi's attention to the fact that a boy in the crowd had five small loaves and two little fish. Jesus made sure the people were seated and ready to participate in a banquet of generous proportions. He thanked His Heavenly Father for the loaves and fish, then distributed them to the people, of whom around five thousand were men. They all ate their fill, and when they collected up the pieces of food left over, these filled twelve baskets.

Jesus had fed the people with massive generosity. That's what God is like. Paul understood that, too. He told the believers in Philippi that God would be sure to meet all their needs according to His glorious riches in Jesus the Messiah (Philippians 4:19). When the people who had been fed became aware of this miraculous sign, the fourth in John's Gospel, they recognized He was the long expected Prophet like Moses who would appear on the scene. This refers back again to Scripture (Deuteronomy 18:15, 18). Not surprisingly, they wanted to make Him King.

As human beings, we have all kinds of needs, don't we? Some of these are spiritual, physical, financial or emotional. Now of course, God wants us to become more holy, and to grow in our understanding of Him, and of what good decision-making looks like day by day. He doesn't want us to repeatedly make daft decisions that will be likely to lead to less than helpful outcomes. There are times, however, when, through no particular fault of our own, we end up in a real predicament, and we can't imagine how we could ever get ourselves out of it. On other occasions, we end up in a pickle precisely because of intentional, sinful, choices we might make. The fact is that God isn't limited by things that limit us. And He can find a way out of our difficulties when, to the human eye, there seems no way forward at all. That being so, there is never a time when we can't trust in Him. He is always generous, and He doesn't believe that good things are bad for us, so we shouldn't have them. Jesus knew our Heavenly Father to be the God of the "how much more" (Matthew 7:11). So can we.

Out For a Stroll on the Sea of Galilee
Read John 6:16-24

It's always nice to go out for a stroll. In today's reading, however, Jesus takes this to another level. As the story begins, His rabbinic disciples get into a boat and start to head across the Sea of Galilee for Capernaum, their base on its northern shore. This is the more conventional way to make the trip, it has to be said. By now it's dark, and, mid journey, a storm whipped up and the sea started to get unsettlingly choppy.

Their fear doesn't subside at all when they see Jesus walking towards them on the lake. He announces His presence and they realise that something divine is going on. When they felt able, His disciples invited Him into the boat, and immediately the craft arrives at their northern destination. This happening, together with their Rabbi walking on the water, demonstrates that at the end of the day, God has the final word. Our understanding doesn't have the final word, and neither does our ability to describe what we know. Some things defy description. And with our eternal God, who stands outside time and space yet is active within it, we needn't be too surprised. The One who spoke Creation into existence (Genesis 1:1-2:3) isn't limited by it. This is the fifth miraculous sign Jesus performs in John's Gospel.

Between verses 22 and 24, we are told that the multitude of people who had been taught by Jesus on the east side of the Sea of Galilee, now realise where He and the disciples are. They duly follow Him to Capernaum, but presumably by the more usual route.

So many members of the community of which Jesus was part, loved and followed Him. They loved His teaching, both how it took their Scriptures with utmost seriousness, and how He managed to apply them in a fresh yet authoritative way. That's why they journeyed to Capernaum. We have to admire their commitment. Wherever He was, they wanted to be. How they and the disciples filled their day shows how seriously they took Him.

That really is a difficult thing. Our diaries and personal planners tend to be filled with so many things. Many of these are unavoidable and truly necessary. How we plan the rest of our time, though, is up to us to a greater extent. True, we need down time, and we should never beat ourselves up for God. That said, it's easy to allow huge amounts of time to slip through our fingers. At the end of many years on spiritual auto-pilot, we can still end up pretty much where we were before we set out on our journey of faith in God.

Now, it might be that He doesn't want us to make great changes to what we are involved in at the moment. We mustn't confuse impetuosity with commitment. However, there might be changes the Lord actually does want us to make. And Scripture reading, prayer, and the wise counsel of godly friends can be a real help here. Whatever the future holds for us, if following Him is our heart's desire, we won't go far wrong.

Difficult Teaching

Read John 6:60-71

These days, easy teaching is often embraced. More difficult teaching can be rejected as not worth the effort. This is especially the case when a particular approach to faith promises much, demands little, and is easy-peasy to understand. Teaching which is demanding and difficult to understand is much more prone to encourage short term believers to reject it and move on. They might be into it today, but they're likely to be into something else tomorrow. We are told in verse 60 that the teaching the Rabbi gave came into the latter category. It was hard to understand, as teaching about eating the flesh and drinking the blood of the teacher is guaranteed to be.

The things Jesus had just taught were always going to divide opinion. In verse 32, He had told the people about how His Heavenly Father had fed their ancestors with bread from Heaven through Moses.

He develops this further by saying that He Himself has come down from Heaven as well, and is the bread of life. When we feed on Him, we live forever. Of the multitudes of descendants of Abraham, Isaac and Jacob who heard Him teach, many found it just too much and walked away. Many more did not, and stuck with it. They continued to follow the Rabbi, and would all the way to the end. He really divided opinion, that's a fact. Even one of His rabbinic disciples would reject Him (verses 70-71), but the other eleven would not.

In today's reading, Jesus again taps into the kind of thing found in Genesis chapter 1 (verses 1 and 2). It is the Spirit of God, or, in Hebrew, the Ruah, which gives life. Jesus had taught about this in John chapter 3 when He was in rabbinic debate with Nicodemus, a senior Judean rabbi. We only really have life in God through the Spirit; and we only really want to receive the Spirit if the Father leads us to Jesus (verse 65). All of this is so obviously difficult to understand. It really is hard. But Peter spoke for the disciples when he affirmed that eternal life is only found in Jesus. He is the Holy One of God (verse 69).

Say what you like about the Scriptures, however long we've been believers, there's always more to learn as we study them. We never come to the point where we think we've exhausted their content, and can safely graduate onto something else. Well, not if we want to take Jesus seriously, anyway. We can be the youngest child and can benefit from hearing about the stories found in Scripture. Or we can be the most mature believer, perhaps even with a Ph.D. in Biblical Studies, and there still much to be gained from ongoing study. What we have already gained from the Bible is true today, and it always will be. As we become more mature in our faith, however, we will be able to understand these truths more completely. And we can increasingly realise how we can live day by day in the light of what we have learnt.

It's a good thing to keep on reading, thinking and praying. When things seem hard, and so difficult to understand, let's push on through to greater understanding. Peter said that the disciples both believed and knew about Jesus with real assurance. Similar confidence and assurance can be ours, too.

Keeping a Low Profile
Read John 7:1-13

Jesus knew how to enter the city of Jerusalem without causing a disturbance or getting Himself arrested by the authorities. What we refer to as the Triumphal Entry was the exception. In the Triumphal Entry, the Galilean Rabbi made the biggest of big splashes, and He knew He was setting in motion a series of events which would lead to His execution by the Romans.

Apart from this, Jesus will have gone up to Jerusalem perhaps three times a year, most years. He did so to celebrate the Biblical Feasts of which we read in Leviticus 23. Most of the time, then, He would simply have seemed like one Rabbi amongst many, up in the big city with His rabbinic disciples. There were no fanfares, and no arrest. In today's reading, however, we read about something quite different even from His normal practice.

By now, John has already started to describe for us the escalating tensions between this Rabbi from the north of Israel and the Judean authorities. In a sense, when our translations tend to refer to "Jews" in verses 1 and 13, it might be better for us to think, instead, that this is a reference to "Judean religious authorities" not "Jews." It is because of the authorities that Jesus initially seems not to be planning to head south in order to celebrate the Feast of Tabernacles at the Temple with everyone else.

Though most of Jesus' followers were from Galilee, we are not to think that absolutely everyone in Galilee believed in Him, of course. In today's passage, we discover that at this stage, even His own brothers, who were Galilean, really didn't. They seem to be goading Him to go south so that more and more important people amongst the Judean establishment could come to believe in Him. And at first, Jesus seems to want to stay put at home when His brothers made the trip.

Later on in this reading, though, Jesus does end up deciding to go to the Feast after all. This time, it wouldn't be with the fanfares and celebration of the later Triumphal Entry. It wouldn't even be a trip made with His disciples in the usual way. No, this time He would go privately, as verse 10 makes clear. It wouldn't be until half way through the Feast that this would change. Only then would He decide finally to go into the Temple courts and start teaching the people (verse 14). The decision to keep a low profile in Jerusalem at first might have been costly for Jesus. His brothers had mocked Him for the very thought that He might go up to Jerusalem without drawing attention to Himself. This semi private visit will have been embarked upon perhaps with their taunts ringing in His ears.

Sometimes, deciding not to raise our own profile and draw attention to ourselves can be costly, especially if so many other people in our friendship circles seem to be doing precisely this about themselves. We might help someone, and not tell anyone about it. We might, again, begin to do something else that's quite significant for God without announcing it. It can be tempting to draw attention to ourselves so everyone can know. But others don't always need to know. Jesus teaches that the important thing is to be assured that our Heavenly Father, who sees what we do in secret, already knows, and He will reward us (Matthew 6:4). Nothing else really matters. Not everybody needs to know. Keeping a low profile can be the right thing to do.

A Very Heated Debate
Read John 7:14-24

Halfway through the Feast of Tabernacles, the Rabbi from Galilee begins to teach publicly in the Temple complex. We read about this festival, which was called Sukkot in Hebrew, in Leviticus 23:33-44. At root, this was a celebration of God's provision for the Children of Israel when they were in the wilderness. As Jesus begins to teach, many of the locals were amazed and thrilled at his understanding (verse 15). For reasons we mentioned yesterday, we think of them as "Judeans" rather than anything else.

What begins here, though, is a sustained and prolonged debate. Sometimes this is between Jesus, on the one side, and some Judeans on the other. At other times it's between Him and members of the Judean authorities on the other. Things get really heated; we can hardly miss that. Some think Jesus is demonically possessed (7:20), and, later, He returns the complement (8:44). As we recently noted, Jesus really divided opinion.

A healing that He performed in chapter 5, the third sign John's Gospel records, is still a bone of contention between this northern Rabbi and the southern authorities. They clearly disagree about how to celebrate the Sabbath, and what was acceptable behaviour on this holy day. Jesus' thinking and practice obviously take the Jewish Scriptures seriously. For example, in them we find teaching Moses gave about the earlier rite of circumcision (verses 22-23). This can be carried out on the Sabbath without any problem. So, Jesus reasoned, someone can be healed on the Sabbath, like the man in John 5, without any problem, too. That's how He saw it. Almost certainly, many members of the community in Galilee would have agreed with Jesus' thinking. The authorities further south, however, saw things very differently. They seem to have been more rigorous on religious matters than their brothers and sisters in Galilee.

The thinking of Jesus was based on the stable foundation of His understanding of the Scriptures. Even though this triggered a very heated exchange between Himself and some teachers from Judea, Jesus was not unsettled by any of this. In many respects, what He modelled seems to be in harmony with His own teaching in the Sermon on the Mount (Matthew 7:24-27). There, He spoke about the difference between the stability of those whose lives are built on the foundation of His understanding of Scripture, and those whose lives are not, and are like an accident waiting to happen.

Most certainly, whatever we do, some will love us, some might dislike us, and some aren't bothered one way or the other. In respect of those who don't agree with our beliefs and practice, we need to know why we do what we choose to do. That being so, we need to know that our lives are really rooted in God, and in His Word. And as we look at the life and practice of Jesus, He most certainly practised what He preached.

Living Water

Read John 7:37-39

So far in John's Gospel, we have found Jesus teaching the people that if they value the writings Moses gave, these really do point to Him. A high view of the Scriptures from Moses and the Prophets would lead people to turn to Him quite naturally. This argument is bubbling along in the background, here in today's verses, too. John chapter 7 is about affirming the Biblical Feasts, about which we read in Leviticus 23, and allowing Jesus to really bring them to life. God's teachings will then be written deep within, and this will celebrate the renewed covenant God makes with His people, the House of Israel and the House of Judah (Jeremiah 31:31-34).

These assumptions are found in today's reading, as we've mentioned. The people are in Jerusalem to celebrate God's provision in the wilderness to their ancestors. This feast of Tabernacles required people to set up temporary shelters (Hebrew: Sukkot) across the city so they could dwell in them. These shelters would obviously, then, help them to identify with those who had done the same centuries before, when Moses led them out of Egypt. But something else happened at this festival as well.

As part of the celebration, a priest would go to the Pool of Siloam in order to draw water. He would then bring it back to the Temple. Jesus Himself draws on the symbolism of this, and invites His hearers to make the appropriate response. Echoing earlier Scripture (Isaiah 55:1), He invites those who are thirsty to come to Him. He will be sure to give them the living water of the Holy Spirit. We'll remember that this was the same offer He made to the Samaritan lady at the well in chapter 4 of this Gospel. But now Jesus, the Messiah, is at the Temple and what He offers the people also echoes the promise God gave to Ezekiel in chapters 47-48 of his book. In the Messiah, there will be streams of water flowing out from the Temple.

Jesus loved the Scriptures; someone who hated them wouldn't have spent so much time applying their message to daily life. It's wise for us to do the same. We read, we pray, and we come to Him to receive God's Spirit. What's set up by this becomes a virtuous circle. In the Spirit we love the Bible more and more. That being so, we instinctively study these writings, we come to Him and are nourished and renewed by Him. These are the good spiritual choices it's always wise to make. The Scriptures and the Spirit belong together, and they always move us further along the path God stretches out for us.

Moses, Mercy and New Beginnings
Read John 7:53-8:11

What an amazing reading today's is. Perhaps like me you find it difficult to separate it from the things we've heard about it over the years. That being so, let's try to delete some of the overlay, about the merciful Jesus and the unmerciful people of His day.

In order to help us do that, we'll need to listen briefly to things said by those who are familiar with the world in which the Rabbi lived and taught. We get the strong impression from the Gospels that though Jesus shared so many beliefs with the Pharisees, He didn't formally study with them. He was far from unlearned, however, as He would have been one of the few people in His society who could read and write (Colleen Conway, The New Oxford Annotated Bible, p. 1535). This is borne out by the fact that in this encounter with some teachers from Judea, He stooped down and wrote on the ground. This, Kent Dobson tells us (The NIV First-Century Study Bible, p. 1355), was possibly "a physical allusion to Jeremiah 17:13 'Those who turn away from you will be written in the dust.'" He also reminds us that, as a group, the Pharisees "possibly didn't support capital punishment," and, anyway, for adultery, the Romans wouldn't have countenanced such a punishment, according to Adele Reinhartz (The Jewish Annotated New Testament, p. 193).

John's story isn't about bloodlust, then. It is located in the middle of the sustained argument about how to understand the teaching of Moses, in chapters 7 and 8 of the Gospel. A woman was brought to Jesus. She had been committing adultery, though the man who was with her must have avoided capture; either way, he wasn't brought. The teaching of the Torah of Moses (Leviticus 20:10; Deuteronomy 17:7; 22:22) defined this as sin. Though the death penalty was no longer imposed for it, the teachers wanted to know whether this northern Rabbi agreed with Moses. Was He "sound" in His understanding of Moses?

What Jesus does is to also cite another Scripture, from Jeremiah. This shines a light upon the sin of those who brought the woman. He doesn't deny that she sinned – in fact He tells her to stop sinning in this way – but He teaches that only the sinless could demand the death penalty for it. And those who brought her are not sinless; in fact, He has written their names in the dust as those whose hearts are not in step with the heart of God. The teachers melt away into the crowd. What Jesus does is to affirm both the teaching of Moses and God's mercy to the lady who stood before Him.

We get the strong impression that Jesus both loved the Scriptures so much, and He understood the Father's purpose in giving them to us.

He understood the big picture of Scriptural teaching, and He could apply the detail of it to daily life. This He did with authority and mercy. We shouldn't be surprised about this. We remind ourselves that the thinking of Jesus itself was shaped by the Scriptures which He heard read at synagogue from boyhood Sabbath by Sabbath.

There's something pretty dreadful about people wielding the Scriptures at others as they rage against their wickedness. It is best not to do such a thing. Let's face it, we know we're sinful too. By the same token, there's something entirely appropriate and realistic about us allowing the Word to chip away our own sins, and make us more holy. Perhaps we remember the old story about the sculptor standing before a block of marble. He wants a horse to emerge from it, so chips away everything that doesn't look like a horse. God wants holiness to emerge in us. Let's allow the Scriptures, in all their beauty, to chip away everything in us that doesn't look like Jesus.

Many Believe in Jesus
Read John 8:12-30

We mentioned back in chapter 7 that a sustained and heated debate was beginning between Jesus from Galilee and others from Judea, further south. This would continue through chapter 8. Following John's account of the encounter between Him and the woman caught in adultery, we now return to the debate.

By the end of today's reading (verse 30), many put their trust in Jesus. They hear His words and are convinced that He is faithful to the teaching of Moses. In a way, when Jesus mentions that He is the light of the world (verse 12), even this reaches back to what is found at the beginning of the Book of Genesis. There, God speaks and light becomes a reality. John has already set the scene for the kind of teaching we get in today's verses. At the start of his Gospel, when John also reflects about the beginning of all things, we find Jesus, the living Word of God, and He is identified with light (John 1:1-18).

So, Jesus is the light of the world (see also John 9:5). People are able to believe in Him, because they have received the kind of revelation about Him which makes this kind of trust in Him possible. As this debate continues, however, Jesus knows that the authorities in Judea don't adequately believe in Him. This is because they don't fully accept the authority of the earlier Scriptures (verse 17). These writings are so important to Him, but they are not important enough to them. Perhaps the power of Rome, which gives a measure of stability in Judea, is casting its shadow instead.

Truth to tell, when we trust in something other than God, it becomes difficult to engage with God's teaching. It also becomes hard to see what He's doing in our lives. God draws close, yet we're not aware of it. Those who comprised the authorities in Judea weren't bad people, indeed, at least two of their number, Nicodemus and Joseph from Ramathaim, accept Jesus. We also know that some Pharisees did, too. Those who didn't, again, weren't bad people. They just couldn't see that the authority of Jesus came from His Heavenly Father.

So often in our world, all sorts of things are going on. People who commentate on these have much to say about it all. That's their job.

Being aware of current events is important. But it is even more important not to let what people say drown out what God says in Scripture. However much time we spend watching the news, and reading coverage on our favourite websites, we need to spend even more time listening to God. John, who wrote this Gospel, was obviously well versed in the Scriptures which came from Moses and the Prophets. This meant that when the Messiah came calling for him, he was ready, willing and able to follow Him (Mark 1:19-20). When we spend time studying the Word of God, this is bound to pay dividends, too. The Word shapes our thinking; it also throws its light on our path and tells us what we need to know about how to live (Psalm 119:105). Reading, studying and praying is never time wasted.

Father Abraham Had Many Sons, Many Sons Had Father Abraham
Read John 8:31-41

You might have noticed that the title for today's reflection is from an old children's song. 50 years ago in Sunday School, we didn't worry so much about inclusive language in what we sang. This song came, as you might remember, complete with much sitting down, standing up and turning around. Those were the days. We mention all of this because the theme of today's reading centres on our ancestor Abraham.

When we looked at chapter 4 of this Gospel, we noticed an interesting debate there, too, between Jesus and a Samaritan woman. Both individuals in that exchange saw themselves as descendants of Abraham, Isaac and Jacob. We noticed, in addition to this, that the group to which Jesus belonged had a high view of the Temple and its celebrations. The community of the lady, with whom Jesus was talking, had an extremely low view of everything that happened in Jerusalem. Both, however, looked back to Abraham their father.

We rehearse this here in order to underline that in today's verses, again, both Jesus, and these Judean teachers, knew Abraham was the founding patriarch of their community. Both had a high view of him. Jesus argues, however, that if these Judean teachers really understood their ancestor, they would follow Abraham's example (verse 39). It is their failure to take his example with sufficient seriousness which is at issue, here. This isn't an argument between Christians and Jews, Jesus and religious leaders.

Jesus argues that His partners in this debate are departing from their ancestor's good example, because, by now, they are well on the way to wanting Him dead. Of course, Jesus recognises that they really are descendants of Abraham, too (verse 37). If only they took him seriously enough to follow him. As things developed further and became even more heated, the Rabbi from Galilee calls these Judean teachers demonic (verse 44) returning the insult they had hurled at Him (7:20).

Well, the message in all of this for us is about bringing our lives into close conformity with the claims we make about ourselves. It's so interesting that there can be times when our behaviour can be in direct contradiction to our self-understanding. This is strange but true. As people, we can be an insufficiently attractive advocate for things that are important to us. We love God in His beauty, but we can present a less than beautiful face to the society in which we live. If we are not careful in all of this, we can even unintentionally convey the impression to people that we think we are somehow superior to others. It's as if we think we are more moral than everyone else, though in truth we know we aren't. We can claim that truth is important to us (verse 32), but we can end up losing our freedom in the minutia, the absolute tidal wave of unimportant details that can end up taking our joy.

Regardless of how much Jesus and the Pharisees agreed, they obviously ended up on something of a collision course. Certainly, the Pharisees weren't bad people, far from it. In the things Jesus teaches in their presence, we get the impression that the Rabbi thinks many of them couldn't see the wood for the trees. Now, there's nothing inherently "Pharisaic" about this. And certainly, contrary to the tropes of historic Christian anti-Semitism, there's nothing inherently "Jewish" about this, either. Each and every one of us can end up drowning in the detail of it all, and radiating a negative and unhelpful impression of our faith.

Perhaps we want to love God, and we remember a time when we really did. But whenever we find ourselves starting to think about our superiority over others, whoever "they" happen to be, then the awful truth dawns. We can have lost our way, somewhat. We genuinely want to follow Jesus, whom to know is life eternal. We want to walk in His truth, a truth that is intended to set us free (verse 32). But there's a possibility that we've allowed religious groups, "isms" and "ologies" to demand more of us than He does. Along this road, the spiritual sweetness of living water can slowly become toxic. Let's take seriously the good example of wonderful believers in the past. As we do this, we can continue to live, in Jesus, as those who are children of Abraham, and heirs to all of the good things He has for us (Galatians 3:29).

The Divine Jesus

Read John 8:48-59

We noticed yesterday how important Abraham was, not only in Scripture, but also in the life of the Jewish community in which Jesus lived and taught. This is a theme which He again takes up in today's reading. In verse 56 He tells us about their great ancestor seeing His day and ministry, and rejoicing.

What Jesus says, here, shows that He has a high view of Abraham. But in this teaching, He also refers to Himself as divine (verse 58).

Now, this was too much for these Judean teachers to accept. In verse 59, John informs us about an attempted impromptu stoning of the Rabbi from Galilee that this triggers. However, He manages to slip away from the Temple complex, and presumably melts into the crowd. He would be back at the Temple many times in the future, because the four Gospels describe this as being His natural teaching venue when in Jerusalem.

Eternal life is made possible, for us, when we believe in Jesus. Death and hell are defeated. Our status is changed, as is the way the Father sees us. Paul describes this superbly in his Letter to the Colossians. He puts it like this. "The Father has rescued us from the domain of darkness and transferred us into the kingdom of His much loved Son, in whom we have redemption, the forgiveness of sins" (Colossians 1:13-14). Our salvation is a completed act, because of Jesus' perfect sacrifice for sin. We receive it as a gift, and nothing can be more precious than this.

Another Healing
Read John 9:1-7

In today's verses, John describes Jesus' sixth miraculous sign. He is still in Jerusalem, where so much of the action takes place in this Gospel. As they walk in the city, the disciples notice someone who is blind. They naturally get to wondering why he was unable so see. Was this some kind of punishment visited on him because of his sin, or perhaps, that of his parents? As we remember, the whole matter of the link between someone's sin and that person's punishment was discussed centuries before in the teaching of the Prophets (Ezekiel 18:20). Yet the disciples couldn't help wondering about the nuts and bolts of this man's circumstances. The Rabbi replied that the man's situation wasn't caused by sin at all. Instead, looked at differently, through his condition God would ultimately be seen at work in his life, once he was healed.

What Jesus had to say about this was given in the context of teaching about spiritual light and darkness. This theme isn't only of interest to John in this Gospel. We know, for example, that a community which lived on the shore of the Dead Sea also devoted much time to thinking about light and darkness. Indeed, they believed that before the end of time came, there would be a massive battle between the children of light and the children of darkness. We can understand, then, why the Rabbi from Galilee saw His own teaching and ministry as something which brought light, and rescued a person from spiritual darkness.

Discussion about this continues in our next two readings. This is because John chapter 9 is dominated by a rabbinic debate about the appropriateness of this healing. You see, the healing took place on a Sabbath, and, as we can imagine, there was still something of a heated debate going on at the time about how to celebrate this day of rest. In time to come, this kind of thing would have been seen as having infringed the teaching of Moses. But for now, the debate about such activity obviously still raged, as we'll see tomorrow.

Verse 5 refers to Jesus as the light of the world. John begins his Gospel (1:1-18) with a traditional reflection on the opening words of the Book of Genesis. These opening verses consider the whole matter of light and darkness. For John, this way of understanding things is important. For us it is, too. We recognize that when we come to Jesus we begin to see things spiritually as they really are. Jesus brings this revelation to us from the Father. The lovely hymn Amazing Grace by John Newton uses that image, too. Newton had a conversion experience which made such a difference to his life. Looking back on his earlier years, he would write that then he "was blind," but after meeting Jesus he ended up seeing things clearly.

As believers, we take the message of Scripture seriously, and this is wise. Because of our high view of God's Word, we study it carefully and prayerfully. Again, this is wise. Yet, however much we study its words, phrases and context, it is ultimately God who switches the light on in our heart and mind to give real understanding. He is the One who gives revelation, after all. Jesus is the light of the world. And ultimately, it's in the light He gives that we see and understand.

The Debate Goes On
Read John 9:8-17

Perhaps division of opinion is inevitable when God is at work. In what we read in this passage, we notice that the Pharisees were divided about the Rabbi from Galilee. Verse 16 shows that some of them didn't believe in Him, but others obviously did. We remember that Judeans in the south of Israel, near Jerusalem, were divided about Him as well. We notice how some Judeans were not at all impressed by this Rabbi from further north. Others believed in Him, though. But with opinion divided about Jesus like this, the debate about Him was sure to continue for some time yet.

We get the strong impression in John chapter 9 that the man who was healed, and his parents, took very different journeys in respect of Jesus, too. Verses 18-23 seem to indicate the parents wanted nothing to do with this opinion-dividing Rabbi. Yet, verse 38, from tomorrow's passage, shows the man ending up with real saving faith in Jesus.

All of this took place against a background which was obviously Jewish. We find in verse 22 an interest in the Messiah, or Christ to use the Greek term, who was to come. Could Jesus really be the One? In verse 35 we note that the way Jesus often preferred to refer to Himself was with the term "the Son of Man," something we also find in the Jewish Scriptures (Daniel 7:13). The world of the Gospels was clearly Jewish. And the Jewish world at the time of the ministry of Jesus was highly diverse, with lots of different views on lots of different things. And on these things, debates often got rather heated.

Isn't it significant that we find, for example in verse 16, that some of the Pharisees had reasons for believing in Jesus, and other members of the same religious school had reasons for not. For some, the way Jesus celebrated the Sabbath was substandard, so He couldn't possibly be the Messiah. For others, who were just as learned, the way He celebrated the Sabbath absolutely wasn't an impediment to them believing in Him at all.

I wonder about you and me. When we look at things other people do, do we tend to interpret them in the most positive light possible, or the most negative? What do we tend to do? Whatever our instincts happen to be when we make assumptions about the motives of others, this certainly says something about us.

Perhaps this was a lesson Paul had learnt as well. When he wrote to believers in Philippi (Philippians 4:8), he urged them to focus on good and positive thinking. The truth is that if our mind is full of such thoughts, it will be difficult for us to instinctively lean towards savage criticism of others, especially if the available information about them might also point in a more praiseworthy direction. We certainly can train ourselves when it comes to how we think. Paul encourages us to bring our thinking into line with our faith in Jesus the Messiah (2 Corinthians 10:5). I wouldn't be surprised if as we go on training ourselves in such things, our desire to savage others with the things we say about them will diminish. It's difficult for us to have a good mind and a bad mouth at one and the same time. We can develop a godly mind, and have godly speech. And that really can't be a bad thing, can it?

Belief and Worship

Read John 9:35-41

It's amazing how often the words of Jesus echo the earlier teaching of Moses and the Prophets. Perhaps that shouldn't surprise us. We've mentioned before that Jesus will have been immersed in these Scriptures at the synagogue in Nazareth from boyhood. These will, therefore, quite naturally have shaped His thinking and teaching in later life.

In today's reading we find another example. The Prophet Jeremiah had drawn attention to the lifestyle of the people many centuries earlier (Jeremiah 2:35). He then tells them that it's because they think they're innocent of any sin that the judgement of God is winging its way towards them. In what John gives us in verses 40-41, Jesus tells the people something similar. We read, here, that they are counted guilty of sin before God because they claim that they see clearly. The words of the Rabbi from Galilee seem to overlap quite naturally with the logic of Jeremiah before Him. So often, it's when we know we're sinful and in spiritual need that we find God to be a God of grace. But when we think we're spiritually rather wonderful, and can strut our stuff for others to admire, well, that's another matter.

The man Jesus had healed had ended up finding himself on collision course with some of the religious leaders in Judea. We noted yesterday that some of the teachers who were loyal to the thinking of the Pharisees believed in Jesus, some did not. The newly healed man seems to have fallen foul of the spiritual leadership of those who didn't agree with Him. But the man's spiritual trajectory was altogether different from theirs.

What wonderful words he utters in this reading. Initially, he isn't quite sure of the identity of Jesus (verses 35-38). The Son of Man? Who's that? When he realises something more of the Person of Jesus, he's then able to fully embrace the Saviour. He now genuinely believes in Him, and this naturally leads him to worship. At one and the same time, as we are seeing for ourselves, some in this chapter are moving away from belief in Jesus. Others are moving towards it. And this man arrives at the point of being able to worship Him, without contradicting appropriate belief that there is one God (see Deuteronomy 6:4).

For some folk then and now, people seem to have all sorts of things to say about Jesus. For some, He was something of a poet. For others, a political activist. Yet again, there are those who believe He was some kind of religious reformer. It is sometimes even argued that He embraced the view that everything's OK, in terms of the choices we make, as long as we love others. When we believe what John taught in this Gospel, however, we'll know Him to be someone who was absolutely at home within the Jewish community in which He lived and taught. And on that foundation, we can know Him to be Messiah, Saviour and Lord. The reality of the situation is this: the more we love Him, and the more our worship embraces the beauty of who He is, the greater our view of Him becomes. It even makes absolute sense for us to exclaim "My Lord, and my God" (John 20:28). He is certainly nothing less.

Jesus and the Flock of God

Read John 10:1-10

Earlier today for my devotional reading, the passage I was looking at was Psalm 78. One thing that struck me was the way that Psalm describes King David. Verses 70-72 tell how God chose him and called him from working at the sheep pen. He would end up shepherding God's people, His inheritance, and looking after them with great skill. Scripture also refers to another giant amongst the Children of Israel as a shepherd. In Exodus 3:1 we're told about Moses, that great leader and teacher; he was a shepherd too.

In all of this, we get the impression that God saw His people as His flock, and longed to care for them. Psalm 23 (verse 1) says as much. The Lord is the Shepherd of His flock. What John writes for us today taps back into that imagery. The people of God are His flock, and verse 11, which we will look at tomorrow, underlines that Jesus Himself is their Shepherd.

In what we're looking at, as chapter 10 begins, we get the impression that false shepherds, who are only looking out for themselves, have the effect of damaging and scattering the flock (verse 10). Jesus is different. He intends to lead us into life in all its fullness, the kind of life even death itself can't snuff out.

Centuries earlier, Ezekiel had condemned some of Israel's kings for being like false shepherds (Ezekiel 34:1-10). God will be a genuine, caring Shepherd who wants to gather His people together and lead them into good pasture. When we are missing out on the good things He wants for us, this really matters to God. Jesus comes as the Shepherd-King, the Messiah.

But who are the false shepherds? Well, perhaps in these verses, John is referring to Rome-appointed political leaders who don't care for God's people. There again, he might be thinking more about Judean religious leaders who also are motivated, at least in part, by not rocking the boat and upsetting the Roman authorities. And we can understand both of these, with the Chief Priest being appointed by Caesar. Either way, Jesus really cares for His own when others don't, even though they should.

This means that He really cares for us as well. When we are juggling with real difficulties, we know that we can bring these things to Him in prayer. When we come to the Lord in prayer, and open the Scriptures to hear from Him, we are assured that we aren't annoying Him. We're not getting in the way. It isn't that He'd rather not have to respond to us because He's busy with something else. He wants us to have life, and life in all its fullness. That was true 2,000 years ago. It's true today as well. What a great thing it is to know that the Lord delights in us. Let's delight in Him, too. Delight in Him is never misplaced.

Who Do You Want To Follow?

Read John 10:11-21

These days, we seem to want to follow all sorts of people. Perhaps that's just how we are. We're created with a perceived need to trust in someone greater than ourselves. In principle, that's fine. But we need to be careful when we choose in whose footsteps we're going to plant our own.

Sometimes people want to follow a particular celeb, maybe an actor, sports-person or musician. So many specialist magazines and websites cater for this demand. It's fine, in principle, to have a significant interest in someone. The truth is, however, that even if a person has a great talent at something, they might still be as broken as anyone else.

Their talent may be off the scale, but they can still be as self-obsessed as any other inhabitant of planet earth. And, let's face it, just because a musician might have a wonderful keyboard technique, it doesn't mean their views on politics or ethics are equally praiseworthy. An actor can really be on top of their game, spectacularly so, and yet what they think about one of the great issues of the day can still be motivated by hostility to others. We are created with a need to follow, but we certainly have to be discerning before we hitch the wagon and move in a direction just because it's advocated by someone else.

When we follow Jesus, though, we're on solid ground. He's the Good Shepherd. That means He really does care for us, and what He teaches about our Heavenly Father is spot on too. He certainly does care for us, and He proved it in His death for us, as a perfect sacrifice for sin. And He's such a wonderful Shepherd, even those who weren't originally members of the Jewish community could end up safely following Him (verse 16).

The incomparable Paul wrote about this in his Letter to the Romans. In this he writes about how those of us who didn't have an upbringing in the Jewish community could happily come to worship the God of Israel alongside descendants of Abraham, Isaac and Jacob. This happens when they come to know Jesus. They might never have been familiar with the Scriptures of ancient Israel, but after they came to know Jesus, their Shepherd and Saviour, they could end up with the same love for them that motivated Jesus from early years.

In our society, people have all sorts of views about all sorts of things. They might argue for them with real fluency, and others might find it difficult to pick holes in their argument. It still doesn't mean they're right, though, or that they speak with integrity and can be safely followed. But when we follow Jesus, we can know that He is the way, the truth, and the life, as John tells us (14:6). Let's follow Him with love and real confidence. He is the Good Shepherd after all.

Giving a Good Testimony
Read John 10:22-42

Here, we find Jesus in the Temple complex once more. He was there because it was the Feast of Hanukkah. This celebrated the rededication of the Temple in the Second Century BCE following its desecration by King Antiochus Epiphanes sometime earlier. In today's verses we find that the debate about the identity of Jesus is continuing. Some Judeans are not convinced that He is someone special. They don't equate what they see of Him with the kind of thing they expect from the Messiah.

The Rabbi from Galilee takes issue with them, and tells them that they can hardly be expected to know about this one way or the other. This is because they don't even really take their Scriptures seriously (verse 34). Now, this isn't to say that Jesus is here implying they're not His Scriptures too. The point is that the Gospels show that He takes the teaching of Moses and the Prophets with utmost seriousness. His issue with these particular Judeans is that they don't seem to. So, as we recap, huge numbers of Galileans followed Jesus. Some Judeans did. But here, He is debating with Judeans who are not impressed with Him at all, not one little bit.

As this passage draws to a close, Jesus relocates across the River Jordan. His cousin John the Baptist had ministered there. Now, many local Judeans came to seek Him out. Interestingly, they had a high view of John as well. But they also appreciated the difference between the two cousins. True, they were both teachers, or rabbis. They were prophets, and they called the people to spiritual renewal and recommitment. There the similarities ended, however.

The ministry of John was preparatory, whereas that of Jesus was the main event. Jesus was the Messiah, John repeatedly made clear that he, himself, was not. Jesus performed miraculous signs, and John did not. Having said that, the testimony of John about Jesus was most effective and powerful (verse 41). On the strength of it, many of the locals ended up believing in Jesus, like huge numbers of Galileans did.

What we say about others is so powerful, too. When we speak positively about other people, and highlight all that's good about them, this speaks positively about us. If we routinely trash people, others are never going to accept our spoken witness to Jesus. It will all ring a bit hollow. John the cousin of Jesus drew attention to Him. Chapter 1 of this Gospel makes that clear. And as a result, many ended up believing in Him. It seems to me that when people know us to be truthful and positive about others, they are much more likely to take our testimony about Jesus seriously too.

In effect our message is "It's not all about me; it's all about Him." Perhaps we have had a much more positive effect on people around us for Jesus than we know. Being pleasant and courteous helps. Against that background, when folk see our commitment to Jesus being modelled in practice, this can be so effective. It was for John the Baptist. It can be for us, too.

The Seventh Miraculous Sign
Read John 11:1-16

In his Gospel, John describes seven miraculous signs Jesus performed. In many ways, the one of which we read in chapter 11 is the most significant. That's because this shows the Rabbi from Nazareth raising His friend, Lazarus, from the dead.

We are told that Lazarus was from Bethany near Jerusalem. His sisters Mary and Martha live there too, as we will see tomorrow. Their brother was sick, so the two sisters got a message to Jesus. The assumption, on their part, must surely have been that the Rabbi who healed the sick could heal their brother as well. This isn't an unreasonable assumption to make, it must be said. On hearing the news, Jesus tells the disciples that this illness won't end in death. Rather, by the time this episode ends, the Son of God will be glorified. But the sisters must have wondered about His timing, especially at first.

We can also understand the bemusement of the rabbinic disciples of Jesus when He seems not to be in any hurry to get to His friend. In fact, He stays put for another two days. When He finally tells them that it's time to go to Judea, where Bethany is situated, again they wonder at the wisdom of all of this. They remember that there were some Judeans who wanted to stone Him to death, and they tell Him, as if He must have forgotten. Isn't it great when we think we know more about things than God does?

What's clear is that Jesus doesn't put His safety down to not setting foot in Judea. He knows that trouble can only ultimately come His way when a particular type of spiritual darkness gathers. Then, from the human point of view, danger will come calling for Him. In the meantime, living in His Father's light, He is perfectly safe.

Jesus then tells His disciples that Lazarus is asleep; He needs to go there to wake him up. But they take His words at face value. If he's only asleep, he'll wake up on his own; why go there? Jesus knows that by the time they get to the grave, Lazarus will have been dead for four days (verse 39). He'll really be dead. This seventh miraculous sign is special; someone genuinely dead will be raised from the dead.

Isn't it interesting that Jesus was in no hurry to get to the grave of His friend? He can take His time, because He knows that everything is in His Father's hands, including His own safety. When we make decisions without that sense of being held by God, we can easily be hasty, blunder in, and make daft decisions. We've all been there and got there medal, I'm sure. Having real assurance from God can give rise to better, wiser, decision-making. If God can even be trusted with life and death issues, He can surely also be trusted with the ordinary things that make up our own lives. As Psalm 46 puts it (verses 1 and 11) even when there is trouble, He is always with us as our refuge, our strength and our fortress. We really are safe in Him. There's no reason to doubt it.

Martha and Mary

Read John 11:17-37

By the time John chapter 11 comes to a close, Lazarus will have been raised from the dead. Today's reading in many ways, however, focuses on his two sisters, Martha and Mary. What we read shows how different the two seem to be, though both presumably love Jesus equally. Their brother will have died four days earlier before the action narrated today takes place.

Jesus is now in the vicinity of Bethany, but hasn't arrived at the sisters' house. Mary remains at home, keeping a particular kind of mourning observance for her brother Lazarus. These days this period of mourning now takes seven days and is called Sitting Shiva, "Shiva" being the Hebrew word for seven. Mary, then, remains at home observing a traditional and respectful period of mourning. She has questions, but these can wait. In this time of mourning, she is supported by many local Judean friends. Her sister responded to news that Jesus wasn't far away from the house rather differently, however.

Martha immediately sets off, because there is a conversation she wants to have with her Rabbi. And unlike her sister she isn't prepared to wait. She tells Him that had He arrived more quickly, her brother could have been prevented from dying. Yet, even now she shares her sister's faith in Him (Luke 10:39). And she knows that the Father will answer His prayer on their behalf. The two sisters clearly can't imagine why Jesus delayed His visit, and both make a point of telling Him what was on their heart. Yet in what we read about them in this Gospel, and in the other three, we get the impression that Mary doesn't always chase hither and thither like her sister. However, they equally seem to know that Jesus isn't simply their Rabbi; there is something even more special about Him than that. They were soon to find out how special.

We are all different, there's no doubting that. In many ways, it's good to embrace the kind of character God has given us. It's also good to develop the gifts and talents He has blessed us with as well. We don't all have to be the same, in order to love Jesus equally. Indeed, He has gifted us with unique things, and as we consecrate these to Him, and allow Him to take them and use them for His glory, we will be able to flourish in line with His will. Along this road, we'll also be able to be at home in our own skin, and to have a real sense of peace in God. Mary and Martha were different. And that wasn't a problem to the One who could raise the dead.

Lazarus: Life After Death, Sort Of
Read John 11:38-44

When we talk about life after death, we normally mean believers spending an eternity in Heaven with God. In today's reading, for

Lazarus, it's something else which is described. Lazarus had died. After 4 days, people knew he really was dead. Jesus raises him back to life. After Jesus calls him from his tomb, Lazarus went on to complete a normal, full human life. Then he will have died, been buried, and will have gone to be with God in Heaven.

The tomb of which we read in John 11, then, was only used for a few days. After that, it was empty once more, because Mary and Martha's brother was brought back to life. But if you have visited Larnaca in Cyprus you might have seen another tomb altogether. This is in the church of St. Lazarus, and there are those who believe that this was his final resting place. Either way, after his eventual death, his body will have remained in the tomb. And he will have gone to be with the Lord.

What we find in what John writes here is an accurate description of the way the Jewish community 2,000 years ago buried those who had died. They buried their loved ones carefully because of their belief in the final resurrection of the dead at the end of time. The vast majority of the community in which Jesus lived shared this faith, with the Sadducees being the only exception. It will have been elements of Judean society which were loyal to the Sadducees which will have been particularly unsettled by Jesus raising Lazarus from his tomb (12:10). For that reason, all of this was a problem which could be solved, as they saw it, if Jesus and Lazarus were taken out of the picture altogether.

If some in Judean society saw this miraculous sign as a problem, others did not. Martha, herself a Judean, would end up seeing this miracle differently. Because she would continue believing in Jesus, the raising of her brother would glorify God in a most wonderful way (11:40). When things challenge our worldview, how we respond really makes all the difference.

Sometimes, dark and difficult things come our way. At such times, Jesus invites us to go on believing in Him. When we look back on it all, we can end up seeing God's fingerprints all over the situation, even if we weren't aware of it at the time. And with hindsight, and faith confirmed, we give glory to God.

Quite An Entry
Read John 12:12-19

Jesus knew how to enter the city of Jerusalem without getting Himself arrested and executed by the Romans. From the Four Gospels, we get the impression that He would have been at the Temple to celebrate the 3 Biblical Feasts of Passover, Pentecost and Tabernacles each year (Leviticus 23). It wasn't unusual for Him to lodge outside the city during these visits, for example, somewhere like Bethany (Matthew 21:17-18). It seems that He would have entered and left by one of its gates daily, and on each of these occasions there was no problem for Him.

What we sometimes call the Triumphal Entry was different, and Jesus meant it to be different. This was a public, choreographed, and highly inflammatory event. Intentionally, He borrowed a donkey and entered like a king. He also did nothing to prevent His mostly Galilean followers from using Scriptures which were associated with the coming of the Messiah, Israel's longed-for King like David. They shout Psalm 118:25-26, as He rode in like the King referred to in Zechariah 9:9. None of this happened by accident. And in a city in which there was only room for one source of authority, Caesar, this could only lead to arrest and execution.

Now, in a sense, there are human, political and easy to understand reasons to account for Jesus ending up on a Roman cross. Yet, as we have reminded ourselves before, the real reason He chose this path was to provide a perfect atoning sacrifice for your sins and mine. John will also have underlined this fact earlier on in his Gospel (1:29). For him, Jesus was none other than the Lamb of God, God's chosen sacrifice for the sin of the world. Whoever believes in Him will not perish, but will receive eternal life (3:16).

Let's praise God every day that He is a God of grace who provides such a remedy for sin. Let's thank Him for leading us to the point of faith in His Son. Let's also go on praying for our loved ones who wouldn't yet even claim to believe in Him. That's why John wrote about Jesus in the first place (20:31). God longs for their salvation even more than we do. That being so, we go on playing our part – living and speaking wisely in their presence, and praying for them in their absence. And let's trust the Lord to do the rest, however long it takes.

God Speaks

Read John 12:20-36

God speaks. We're not surprised by this, because a Jewish and Christian understanding of Scripture is built upon the foundational belief that these writings are God's Word. He has spoken definitively through them, and will never contradict His divine revelation. It is equally true to say that He has also definitively spoken through His Son, Jesus. Through His teaching, we know Him to be the living Word. God will never contradict what He has spoken through His Son either.

In addition to this, it was not unknown within the Jewish community to believe that God also spoke directly and audibly from Heaven. One example of this is found in Exodus 19:16-19 in the account of God speaking to Moses on Mount Sinai. Another example is found in accounts of Jesus' immersion in water at the hands of His cousin, John (Mark 1:11).

John taps into that kind of Biblical imagery when he tells us today about Jesus praying to His Father about the ordeal He will soon face (verses 27-28). In response, God speaks to His Son (verses 28-29) through an audible voice. And this thunderous, divine, voice, according to Jesus, was for the benefit of the people who heard it (verse 30). God is a God of glory, as well as a God of grace. He is majestic and sovereign. However intimate and close He is to us, and He certainly is in Jesus, we are right never to ignore the Scriptural insight that He is awesome, and over and above us, too.

Day by day, as we live the life God has stretched out before us, we are informed by the things He has said through His Word. God has spoken definitively through the Scriptures given to ancient Israel. He has also spoken through the things that were written by those who followed Jesus, their Saviour and Messiah. There can also be occasions when God will speak through His Spirit, as we find throughout the Acts of the Apostles. Sometimes this takes the form of guidance about who to appoint for a particular task, or what specific steps need to be taken in order that God's will is done in practice. But He will never contradict His Word, the Scriptures. The more familiar we are with them, the more stable our foundation in life will be. We are wise to build on this rock-like foundation, and when we do, we will never go far wrong (Matthew 7:24-27).

Bibliography.

The English Standard Version Study Bible. Crossway Bibles.

The Authorized Version. Cambridge University Press.

The New King James Version. Nelson.

The Third Millennium Bible (New Authorized Version). Deuel.

The New International Version. The International Bible Society.

The Revised English Bible. Oxford University Press, Cambridge University Press.

The New Revised Standard Version. Division of Christian Education of the National Council of the Churches of Christ in the USA.

A New New Testament. Hal Taussig. Mariner Books.

The Tanakh. The Jewish Publication Society. 1985.

The Jewish Study Bible. Ed. Adele Berlin and Marc Zvi Brettler. Oxford University Press.

The Complete Jewish Bible. JNTP

The Jewish New Testament Commentary. David H. Stern. JNTP.

The Authorized Daily Prayer Book of the United Hebrew Congregations of the Commonwealth. Fourth Edition. Collins, London.

Forms of Prayer for Jewish Worship, volume 1. Reform Judaism, London.

Siddur Lev Chadash. Liberal Judaism, London.

Principles of Jewish Spirituality. Sara Isaacson. Thorsons.

Judaism—a Short Introduction. Lavinia and Dan Cohn Sherbok. Oneworld, Oxford.

Judaism—a Short History. Lavinia and Dan Cohn Sherbok. Oneworld, Oxford.

Israel—a History. Martin Gilbert. Black Swan.

myjewishlearning.com

earlyjewishwritings.com

Prayer Book – In Accordance With the Tradition of the Eastern Orthodox Church –
All Saints of Alaska. Kindle Edition.

The Septuagint – translated Sir Lancelot C.L. Brenton. Kindle Edition.

The Tanakh. The Jewish Publication Society 1917. Kindle Edition.

Hitler's Willing Executioners. Daniel Jonah Goldhagen. Abacus.

Jerusalem: the Biography. Simon Sebag Montefiore. Pheonix.

Jerusalem: the Making of a Holy City. Simon Sebag Montefiore. BBC4.

The Expositor's Greek Testament – Biblehub.com

The Jewish Encyclopedia (cited by D.H. Stern, The Jewish New Testament Commentary).

biblicalhebrew.com./nt/beatitudes

The Contemporary Torah. David E.S. Stein, Adele Berlin, Ellen Frankel and Carol L. Meyers. Jewish Publication Society.

The Restored New Testament. Willis Barnstone. Norton.

The Jewish Annotated New Testament. ed. Amy-Jill Levine and Marc Zvi Brettler. Oxford University Press.

The New Oxford Annotated Bible (4th edition). ed. Michael D. Coogan. Oxford University Press.

The Misunderstood Jew. Amy-Jill Levine. HarperOne.

Short Stories by Jesus. Amy-Jill Levine. HarperOne.

The Complete Jewish Study Bible. ed. Rabbi Barry Rubin. Hendrickson Bibles.

Gods and Kings: Chronicles of the Kings, Book One. Lynn Austin.

Song of Redemption: Chronicles of the Kings, Book Two. Lynn Austin.

The Strength of His Hand: Chronicles of the Kings, Book Three. Lynn Austin.

Faith of My Fathers: Chronicles of the Kings, Book Four. Lynn Austin.

Among the Gods: Chronicles of the Kings, Book Five. Lynn Austin.

Return to Me: the Restoration Chronicles, Book One. Lynn Austin.

Keepers of the Covenant: the Restoration Chronicles, Book Two. Lynn Austin.

NIV First-Century Study Bible. Kent Dobson. Zondervan Bibles.

The Gospel According to John (I-XII). Raymond E. Brown. Anchor Bible Commentaries vol. 29.

The Gospel According to John (XIII-XXI). Raymond E. Brown. Anchor Bible Commentaries vol. 29a.

The Epistles of John. Raymond E. Brown. Anchor Bible Commentaries vol. 30.

Reading Romans Within Judaism. Mark D. Nanos. Cascade Books.

Reading Paul Within Judaism. Mark D. Nanos. Cascade Books.

Reading Corinthians and Philippians Within Judaism. Mark D. Nanos. Cascade Books.

The Irony of Galatians. Mark D. Nanos. Augsburg Fortress.

The Mystery of Romans. Mark D. Nanos. Augsburg Fortress.

Paul Within Judaism. Edited by Mark D. Nanos and Magnus Zetterholm. Fortress Press.

Paul Was Not a Christian. Pamela Eisenbaum. HarperOne.

Invitation to Romans. Pamela Eisenbaum. Abingdon Press.

Reinventing Paul. John G. Gager. Oxford University Press.

Paul the Pagans' Apostle. Paula Fredriksen. Yale University Press.

Paul the Jew. ed. Gabriele Boccaccini and Carlos A. Segovia. Fortress Press.

The Message of Paul the Apostle Within Second Temple Judaism. ed. Frantisek Abel. Fortress Academic.

Maccabean Martyr Traditions in Paul's Theology of Atonement. Jarvis J. Williams. Wipf and Stock.

The Gnostic Gospels. Elaine Pagels. Vintage Books.

Beyond Belief. Elaine Pagels. Vintage Books.

biblejourney.org

The Orthodox Study Bible. Thomas Nelson.

The Gnostic Bible (revised edition). Willis Barnstone and Marvin Meyer. Shambhala Publications Inc.

Lost Scriptures. Bart D. Ehrman. Oxford University Press.

The Real Paul. Bernard Brandon Scott. Polebridge Press.

The Authentic Letters of Paul. Arthur J. Dewey, Roy W. Hoover, Lane McGaughy and Daryl D. Schmidt. Polebridge Press.

patheos.com

biblical archeology.org

jewsforjudaism.org

theos-sphragis.org

jewishvirtuallibrary.org

The Apocrypha and Pseudepigrapha of the Old Testament, Volume 2. Robert Henry Charles. Apocryphile Press.

The New Testament. David Bentley Hart. Yale University Press.

Also by Martyn Perry:

Wisdom for Living

Also found on Amazon

Printed in Poland
by Amazon Fulfillment
Poland Sp. z o.o., Wrocław

60931665R00096